# THE MANAGER'S DILEMMA

## ASAF MORAG

Producer & International Distributor
eBookPro Publishing
www.ebook-pro.com

**The Manager's Dilemma**
Asaf Morag

The first version was published in Israel in November 2019
Translation from the Hebrew by Itamar Toussia Cohen

Contact: asaf@rakia-eng.co.il
ISBN 9798683721107

# THE
# **MANAGER'S DILEMMA**

HOW TO SET "GAME RULES" THAT WILL
MAKE ALL PARTICIPANTS WORK FOR THE
PROJECT

PROJECT MANAGEMENT ACCORDING
TO THEORY OF CONSTRAINTS & GAME
THEORY

# **ASAF MORAG**

# Contents

Acknowledgments...................................................................7

**PART 1** | CONFLICTS OF INTEREST

1. Time Is Money .......................................................9

2. Things Could Always Be Worse ....................................... 13

3. The Consultant's Conflicts of interest............................ 22

4. The Subcontractor's Conflict of Interests...................... 30

5. The Designer and Owner's Own Conflicts of interest.. 40

6. Conflicts of interest Between a Player and His Team ... 47

7. Even the Owner Answers to Someone,

With Their Own Conflicts of interest................................. 54

8. The Environmentalists' Interests...................................... 64

9. Better Claim Than Work.................................................... 71

10. Sally Erikson.................................................................... 80

11. The Designer's Interests ................................................. 84

**PART 2** | THE GOAL FUNCTION

12. Chambers' Vision............................................................ 92

13. The Owner's Take on Reality ........................................ 99

14. Red-Handed ................................................................. 107

15. Jayden's Dilemma.......................................................... 111

16. Critical Path and Critical Chain ................................. 116

17. Solving Jayden's Dilemma ...................................... 127

18. Game Theory and the Prisoner's Dilemma ................ 133

19. Why Is a Goal Function Necessary? .......................... 141

20. Unlocking the Goal Function .................................... 156

21. The Road Can Be Hastened ...................................... 166

22. Meeting the Demands of the Law ............................. 172

## PART 3 | THE MANAGER'S DILEMMA

23. Eli Goldratt or John Nash ........................................ 177

24. The Client's Client .................................................. 184

25. Everyone Has a Goal Function .................................. 189

26. A Family Prisoner's Dilemma .................................... 203

27. The Client's Own Constraints .................................. 211

28. Applying the Goal Function ...................................... 215

29. Resolving a Family Prisoner's Dilemma ..................... 225

30. No Info, No Win .................................................... 230

31. Rewiring a Mindset ................................................ 240

32. Fixing the Contracts ............................................... 249

33. The Israelis .......................................................... 260

34. Applying the System ............................................... 270

35. Family ................................................................. 280

Epilogue .................................................................. 284

## ACKNOWLEDGMENTS

Like any other project, this book is the product of great efforts made by many different people who, each in their own way, contributed to it, and to whom I would like to give thanks. In particular, I wish to thank those who read the manuscript and offered hundreds of useful comments and insights, ranging from grammatical corrections to debates about the professional or literary composition of the book, some of which prompted me to make substantive changes to its content.

To my friends at Netivey Israel, the National Roads Company of Israel, the finance people—Director of the Budgets Department Elad Aloni, and Ariel Chaimon who shed light on the budgetary and financial aspects of the book, and added invaluable insights from the field of game theory. The operations people—Deputy Director-General of Railways Zachi Gura and Director of the Engineering Wing Amir Deckel, who contributed from their vast experience of both large and small projects in various organizations, both from the perspective of the contractor and from the perspective of the owner. To the information systems man, Amir Laor, who added useful comments regarding the information problem presented in the book. The schedule consultants, Shirly Cohen and Tal Lebanon, who offered hundreds of useful suggestions to improve and enhance the language employed in the book. To Uri Friedlander and Yoav Sarne, who contributed from their wealth of experience as owners of project management companies. To Dr. Israel Lerner, who made his experience in managing projects in the fields of silicon fabs available to me. To my sisters, Adi Eilat and Meirav Mitrani, and to my parents, Yigal Morag and Ora Eilat, who helped focus my attention on professional concepts that needed illuminating for the lay reader. To Daniel Hadar, who challenged the logic and validity of some of the questions I asked and the answers I proposed. To Ido Mann for several enlightening conversations. To Ilan Sharoni for illustrating the cover and making insightful comments on the manuscript. To Erez Feigenberg for his helpful marketing advice and to Shimon Yanai, for comments on the wording of the text. To Liat Hadar-Mann for the countless literary comments that forced me to rewrite entire sections, until muddled explanations were made lucid, and exhausting passages made fluent. To Arnon Dominitz, my writing partner, who had to stand seeing his writing edited time and time again, until it successfully conveyed the ideas I asked of him to refine. And above all else, to my wife, Yael Mann-Morag, for the countless conversations, comments on my writing, and for simply being herself—without her, bringing this book to light would not have been possible.

To all of you—thank you from the bottom of my heart.

**Asaf Morag**

# PART 1 | CONFLICTS OF INTEREST

## 1. TIME IS MONEY

Ethan McKay looks exhausted as I sit down in his office at 9 a.m. Two empty coffee cups on his desk and the concerned look in his eyes reveal that something is wrong. His five o'clock shadow, the mass of paperwork sprawled across his desk, and an empty whiskey glass are a giveaway that it's probably serious. Ethan is the type who keeps a clean shave and a neat desk. He is also not one to mix coffee and whiskey.

"Good morning, Eric," he says. "Do you know why I called you in?" he uncharacteristically skips the small talk.

Even though all I got from his secretary was a text message with Ethan's name and a time for the meeting, I think I know. "Is it the 612?"

"Yes, the 612. If we keep going at this pace, this project's going to drive the company into the ground. Thompson's a good guy, but he can't get it up and running. We need to replace him."

"I thought the last few weeks were better. What happened? Why replace him now?"

"I don't have deep enough pockets to let him learn at his own leisure. Ten months in, we're already four months behind schedule. The financial repercussions are devastating."

He slides over a piece of paper with some numbers scribbled on it. The important part is underline in red ink at the bottom: **Fine for failure to deliver the project by the**

**agreed-upon date: 1% of project's value per each month's delay**. That's $1M per month over four months. The math is simple.

We work in a line of business where the average profit is about 4%. We were willing to go way below average this time, because of this project's strategic value. Laying down 14 miles of road for Highway 612 was a tall order to begin with, but that was exactly why we wanted it so bad. This project could propel us to the big leagues. We needed a high-budget job under our belt to meet the requirements for bidding on the big-money projects. That's why we were willing to bid so low for the contract. However, when your projected profit is $1.5M to start with, taking a $4M hit is no small matter. If you add the overhead costs for these extra months – you could see why Ethan was worried.

I didn't realize things were this bad. Ethan is in charge of the project himself, and I only visited the site on a couple of occasions since construction started. Thompson gave me a tour and showed me the progress they'd made. Even though I knew they were behind schedule, it felt like things were moving along. There were no earthquakes, strikes, hurricanes, or force majeure of any kind to hold us back. Just the regular snags and hiccups, we couldn't get the permit to start digging on time, and faced some delays by the Water Authority, the Electric Corporation, the Nature and Parks Authority, etc., etc. Nothing we haven't seen a million times before.

However, the numbers don't lie; we're going to be late delivering this project, and we're going to pay for it – big time.

"Do you need to speak with the bank again?" I try to get

a sense of the mess we're in.

"I've already talked to the bank, and other people as well. You remember the figures, right?"

I nod my head. I was the one who drew up the budget for this project, so I know it inside out. Highway 612 is a $100M project – nearly ten times the company's equity capital.

"We are leveraged so heavily on this project that it'll be nothing short of a miracle if we're still on our feet when this thing wraps up. Eric, now's the time to panic."

I knew it. He wants me to chaperone the new project manager. We both know I've got way too much on my plate as it is, and this is supposed to be his project. But how can I say no when things are so dire?

"Sure," I answer without hesitation. "Do you have someone in mind to replace Thompson?"

"Yes," he looks me dead in the eye. "You."

For over twenty years, he's been using this look to get people do what he wants. People in the company joke that he owes his career to that steely gaze.

"Hold on. You don't mean—" he nods his head, never breaking eye contact. "Ethan, I'm working overtime as it is. We agreed I'd be taking less hours, not more."

Ever since the divorce, the exact hour I get back home on days I have the kids has become a thing I can't compromise on. Ethan knows this and has been supportive of me in this regard. Starting next week, I was going to leave the office at 4 p.m. two times a week. That doesn't go hand-in-hand with doubling my workload.

"Eric, we've got no choice. We've made more mistakes than we can afford to make with this project already. I don't have time to wait for some fresh project manager to learn the ropes, until he can get up to speed on the project."

I still can't believe the turn this conversation has taken. I was amusing myself with the idea of changing my work routine anyway, but, since the divorce, I was thinking of the complete opposite. After years of hardly ever seeing my kids, I was ready to decrease my workload – not increase it. I thought about getting out of the contracting sector altogether. I even applied for a government job.

Now that the family was broken up, I realized I wanted to spend more time with the kids before they disappear off to college. I thought I had long-since finished with on-site project management, yet here was Ethan sitting opposite me, asking me to do just that.

"I'm not talking about doubling your workload, Eric. I'll take you off your regular assignments. Why don't you take a day off, talk to your kids, explain to them that this is temporary and that they're not losing you to your job again."

No chief engineer would take kindly to being demoted back to on-site work. Had this been any other boss, I would have simply said no. But Ethan isn't any other boss. I started working for him as a junior engineer, and not only did he show me the ropes, he was like an older brother to me – at times, you could even say he was the father that I never had. It was he who gave Ashley the sombrero that became the first piece in her hat collection, and it was him that I turned to when I first started contemplating divorce.

Long story short, a moment later he was congratulating me on my new role.

## 2. THINGS COULD ALWAYS BE WORSE

I pull up to Tom's Café downtown to pick up Ashley, parking my Toyota Land Cruiser with two wheels on the sidewalk. I can see her smiling through the glass doors as she takes off her black apron and runs out toward me in a short red skirt and light jacket. "Hey, Dad," she gives me a peck on the cheek, while the other waiters look at us through the windows.

Right before the weekend, we're heading up to see the new road. During the drive, she proudly tells me all about the day she's had at the café – her first real job.

We veer off the old road and go past the gate. I can see Ashley smiling from the corner of my eye as I step on the gas and the car clears the mound. "You wanna drive?" I ask her when we reach the paved subbase. "Sure," she answers right away, "that's what I came for!"

We switch places, I'm in the passenger's seat now. "Ready?" I ask as she tucks her hair behind her ears. "Yeah," she replies eagerly. "Pedal to the metal!"

I don't even look at the road – just at her face, intently focused. There's a glint of exhilaration in her eyes as she slaloms around the red marked rods lined in the center of the road. Her excitement is contagious, and for a brief moment, I feel like fifteen years ago when she was my little girl and I took her to ride the horse carousel at the amusement park. She opens the window to let the wind course through her hair, grabs the wheel tightly, and nearly stands up on the gas pedal. The car fishtails at every turn, but Ashley keeps it under control – just like I taught her. The cornfields on either side of the road become a green blur. I turn off the radio, to revel in the sound of the engine roaring and the tires screeching as they skid on the subbase. I'll be the last to deny that working on-site has its benefits.

"How far did they get?" she turns to face me, and immediately looks back at the road.

"You've got about another mile to go nuts," I say.

She eases her foot off the gas and catches her breath as we can see the end of the road rapidly approaching. A red blur becomes a compactor; another one just after it slowly sharpens into a giant yellow excavator. We see Kevin's trailer as well.

Ashley stops the car just a few feet away from the mound and forcefully pulls the hand-brake. "That was awesome!"

Work grinds to a halt. A couple of construction workers turn to look over at us, and the compactor driver kills the insufferably loud engine. Only the excavator, about 200 feet away from us, carries on with his work. With a spring in her step, despite wearing sneakers scandalously unfit for a construction site, Ashley joyfully skips over holes in the ground and other obstacles, the sweet scent of her perfume mixing with the putrid odor of the sweaty, dusty workers. She gayly smiles at everyone who is looking at her – that is to say, *everyone*. I put on my best *you better watch it!* face. But they can all see how proud I am to call this little beauty my own, and are wholly unbothered by the stern, intimidating look I'm trying to pull off.

Kevin is already standing there. Somehow, he manages to

look elegant even with a pair of rough jeans and work boots. For as long as I've been working for Rhombus, this guy has been my go-to site manager for important projects. He just knows what he's doing. If everyone in America would work as efficiently as Kevin, there would be no such thing as a delayed project. Maybe not everything would be perfectly constructed, but you could bet your life it would be done on time. So just imagine, even with Kevin's efficiency, we're still far behind…

Rodriguez, the planner's representative, pulls up with his black Chevrolet Silverado. He gets out of the truck to shake my hand. His cowboy hat and shiny Ray-Ban sunglasses make him look like an adventure travel catalogue model, but he knows the job. It's no coincidence Danielle picked him as her representative for this project. "Good week, Price," he half asserts half asks. "It's not over yet," I respond, and everyone cracks up. Some of them, at least, aren't just sucking up.

"Someone up there's looking out for you," he looks up to the clear blue sky. At this time of the year you never know what kind of weather you'll get. This year it couldn't have been any better, no storms, hardly any snow, mostly clear skies that let us get on with our work. Colleagues of mine who work up north like to joke that the most important guy on their team is the weatherman.

We pack into the Silverado with Rodriguez, and head over to the trailer to review the previous day's plans and correspondence.

"Whoa!!"

We all turn our heads to Rodriguez, who rattled the truck with his shout.

"Holy shit!" he goes on, pointing toward the excavator on the side of the road ahead of us.

"What's the matter?" I ask him, trying to understand what's getting him so worked up. Rodriguez floors it without answering. "I think he hit something."

Every possible scenario, as well as some impossible ones, feverish run through my head in the twenty seconds that lapse until we reach the excavator. Communications line, sewage pipe, water line, indigenous burial ground, the cadaver of some poor guy the mafia buried… We leap out of the truck and cross the short distance to the excavator, whose operator pops out of its yellow door looking shaken to the bone. "Fucking shit!" Kevin yells. I had never heard him swear before. "Just don't tell me it is what I think it is."

The two managers, driver, and I are standing over the hole in the ground. None of us bother looking over at the other guys. We all know what's going on. Through the thin smoke caused by the short-circuit we see a jumble of thick lacerated cables and exposed lines. No one utters a word. Rodriguez looks up at the sky again, a completely different expression on his face this time. Only Ashley, who has rushed over to join us in the meantime, doesn't understand what's going on. "What did he hit?" she asks. Kevin looks over me, then at the driver, "High-voltage cable."

The excavator operator, a big guy with graying hair, slowly climbs down. I run over to him, make sure he's okay, and bellow, "What the hell are you doing digging over here!" He stands in front of me, clearly still dazed from the blast. I grab him by the shoulders – he's older than me, and probably stronger as well, but I'm hell-bent, "Why did you rip the cable?" I insist loudly. He doesn't even try to resist; he just stares at me blankly. A couple of seconds later, he points to the ground just up the ditch. "You see?"

I do see. Dozens of neatly lined metal rods protruding from the ground with red marking tape tied to their tips, marking where to dig. Even without measuring, I can see that he dug exactly where he was supposed to. Kevin immediately gets the meaning of this and is already on the phone. I hear fragments of his conversation and understand he's speaking with the electric company. "They're on their way," he quickly informs as he hangs up, "they should have this fixed in three to four hours."

I call him and Rodriguez over to the trailer. It's clear to me that we have to understand exactly how this happened and stick to one story. There'll be enough time to bicker among ourselves later. We're not even at the door yet when our phones ring at the same time, like some sort of coordinated attack. "Price, are you responsible for this?!" the mayor himself is shouting at me. "Electricity's out in four neighborhoods, mine included." "Mayor Johnson, let me explai—" I mumble, but he's not finished, "Is this your way of wishing us a pleasant weekend??" I calculate in my head that a couple of minutes have gone by already, our location is on the electric company's computers, and each department in every municipality around the country can see what's going on on our site. "It doesn't look so bad," I lie. "Good thing it's a nice day out, huh?"

The mayor was in no mood for jokes. "Listen here, I have enough trouble with this road as it is, you better have this thing resolved quick. Got it?"

"Sure thing, sir."

Sure thing? Rodriguez is on the phone and I'm guessing it's Danielle he's talking to. I don't blame her. Brotherly love is well and good, but business is business – every man for himself. Kevin is shouting at someone over the phone, and I ask him to end the call.

We go into the trailer. Five minutes ago, we were each planning our weekends, but now we're in a crisis state of mind. "What are we gonna do about this?" I blurt out, while the two of them pour over the plans. "I don't think it'll take 'em long to fix this," Rodriguez says in a casual voice that irritates me. "I'm not talking about how long that'll take," I angrily reply and step outside.

We don't know anything yet – who's to blame, how long it'll take to fix the damage, or how this is all going to affect our work moving forward – but it's clear that this day, marking exactly one week since I took over the project, is a disaster. I lean back against the trailer wall and clasp my head in frustration. "What's going on, Dad?" I forgot she was here. "What's going on? Well, we don't know yet, but I hope everything's gonna work out," I try to cheer her up, while actually trying to convince myself. She cautiously places a comforting hand on my shoulder, as if I were the child and she the adult. "I spoke with the workers; they all say that this shouldn't take more than a couple of hours to fix." I look at her; the last thing I feel like doing right now is explaining all this to her, but she goes on, "You weren't going to work tomorrow anyway, so maybe it's not so bad after all."

"It's not about fixing this, Ashley. Sure, it's a bit of a head-ache and the mayor's gonna be on our tail for a couple of weeks, but that's not the problem."

"So what is the problem?"

"The problem is that we've hit a high-voltage cable which, theoretically, was supposed to be relocated before construction began, exactly for the purpose that we could lay the road here without hitting it. I don't know the long-term ramifications of this, but it's not going to be good."

"And all this happened because the excavator driver dug where he wasn't supposed to?"

"No. And that's exactly the problem, the operator dug exactly where he was supposed to."

"So, that means the plan was wrong, right?"

"It looks like it. That's why we've got Rodriguez here, his job is to see that everything is going according to plan. We don't know if the problem is the line or the road, but one of them is in the wrong place."

"Okay, but I still don't understand, why is the rest of the road in jeopardy because of just one power line?"

"Because my profit in this project is based on time."

"What do you mean?"

"Forty thousand dollars a day for each day I get this job done ahead of schedule. That goes both ways, of course, and I'm charged for each day I'm late.

"Okay, but are the couple of hours, or even couple of days, it could take to fix this are enough to completely derail this project?

"I wish it were only a couple of hours. Honest to god, if you offered me just one week's delay, I'd take it in a minute."

She looks at me puzzled, not seeing where I'm going with this.

"It's safe to assume we'll need to move the road in this segment or, more probably, the line—and that takes time."

"I get that, but how long would that take?"

"I could have guys come in and do it in three days, but it's not up to me. We're venturing into a jungle of bureaucracy – authorizing plans, coordinating with the electric company, and a hundred other things that could go wrong."

"That doesn't sound like a short time."

"It isn't. I've been in these situations before. This could take up to three months."

"Three months?? That's ninety days!"

I can see on her face she's quickly calculating ninety days times $40,000. We're standing there in silence, waiting for Kevin and Rodriguez to come out of the trailer.

"Don't worry, that's the worst-case scenario. It might turn out to be nothing."

And there's the electric company's white van making its way across the half-paved road. I see it approaching and pray that those guys can clean up our mess quickly.

"See? The electric guys can get things moving quickly."

"Yeah, when there's a blackout and half the city's on their ass. Try talking to them when you want to get your plans approved, then you'll see how fast public corporations actually work. No one over there is in any kind of rush, and they sure as hell don't care about my bonus."

The phone is ringing nonstop, but I don't even bother answering anymore. Rodriguez steps out. "I still don't know exactly what the problem is. The whole country's off for the weekend anyway, I think it's best you call a designers' meeting for Monday morning." Unfortunately, he's right. I was hoping to hear something else, a precise identification of the problem and perhaps even some plan to start working on, but the guy's a professional, he doesn't just wing it.

"Okay, Dad, let's go home. I don't think there's anything left for you to do here." I look at her and, for a second, I envy the young waitress who locks her worries away with the cash in Tom's register at the end of the day. "She's right, Eric," Kevin joins in. "Go home. I'll stay here until they fix it."

# 3. THE CONSULTANT'S CONFLICTS OF INTEREST

We scheduled the meeting for 10 a.m. Usually, that would be around midday on the site, but not today. So far, only Kevin has arrived. We go into his trailer, where he's already laid out snacks and pitchers of orange juice; even when there is no work to do on the site, he still manages to find tasks that need doing.

"You think we'll see your sister here today?" he passes me a basket of pastries he picked up from a bakery on the way over. "I don't think so. Rodriguez is her guy for these types of things. Besides," I say, "I think designers feel more comfortable behind the safety of their office desks than in the field where their drawings materialize. Danielle's no exception. She'll do her best to avoid having a meeting in unfamiliar territory, without easy access to her computer files, her secretary, and the compelling aura of a partner in a high-end firm."

Ignoring my not-so-subtle jibes at my sister, Kevin asks, "Besides Rodriguez, who else is going to be here?"

I pull out my phone and read the email I received over the weekend. "So," I start reading out the names, "Janna Young, the design coordinator from LB; Amy Park, who designed the wall, will represent BDC; and Harrison," I pause to look for his last name, which I can't find in the email, "the electrical designer from Cooper-Barnes. Of course, Bill Blackstone, the Department of Transportation's project manager, is going to be here. They're the ones who commissioned the project and are paying for it."

"Do you think we'll be able to work this out today?"

"I hope so, Kevin. I informed Ethan about what happened, and he was not happy. You know, we all thought we were past the point in this project where we would hit such a stumbling block."

At 10 a.m. sharp, everyone is seated in the trailer. Amy Park is revealed to be an industrious young woman. Janna Young is a woman in her mid-forties. Seated between them, "Harrison" of Cooper-Barnes turns out to be Steven Harrison, whose boyish appearance makes him seem a bit out of place, like a kid in his school's career-day seated between his mother and older sister. The three's neat attire quickly reveals that the field is not their natural habitat. Next to them is Bill Blackstone, who I'd met at the start of the project. Bill is a silver-haired, highly experienced professional, representing the Department of Transportation (DOT) who commissioned of this project; he's the type that doesn't speak much, but when he does, you listen.

Once everyone's settled in, Rodriguez reaches for the refreshments. I start out by thanking them all for coming. "I'm certain we're all fully focused on the same objective, that is, getting this matter resolved as quickly as possible," I see their heads nodding along slightly as I speak. "First matter of business is understanding exactly what happened. Rodriguez, the floor is yours."

Rodriguez takes charge of the meeting. He goes around the table, "Amy, let's start with you. How did you determine the location of the wall?"

"That's simple," she replies. "In this section, the road stretches across the side of a hill, and the wall supports it from one side. The width of the road was determined by the road designer. That plan hasn't been changed at any point, and the road is precisely eighty four feet wide. Our wall is positioned so that its inner edge is forty two feet from the road's center. Add to that the width of the wall, which is one and a half feet at the base, and you get precisely forty three and a half feet, taking into account standard construction deviations. That hasn't changed since the preliminary plans were drawn up."

Us being the contractors, it's clear who she's referring to when she says *standard construction deviations.* But I let it slide. Rodriguez passes the ball over to Harrison, the electrical designer.

"How did you determine the location of the cable?" he asks.

The young man, who hasn't uttered a word yet, suddenly rises to his feet and looks around at us with an incredulous look on his face. "Well?" Rodriguez says, gesturing him to speak.

"Well, what?" he asks to everyone's amusement. Everyone but me.

"Well—why didn't you plan the cable farther? You knew there was going to be a support wall constructed there!"

"You need to understand, Mr. Rodriguez, we worked in strict accordance with the main drawing." He doesn't say it directly, but everyone knows that the main plan is drawn up by the chief designer, whom Rodriguez represents. "As Ms. Park showed before, they marked the wall alongside the road. When we planned the relocation of the cable, we adhered to the standard precautionary distance required." He sees we're not convinced, and adds, "In fact, we went beyond that. We placed the cable three feet away from the wall, even though we could have legally place it right beside the wall."

Rodriguez turns to me, and says, "Well, from the planning perspective things seem to be in order. Could be on the execution side?"

"Hold on a second, let's get this straight," I say in a measured voice. "The wall's designer says she deserves a reward for her work, and the electrical designer says he did his job immaculately." I look around at them, trying my best not to get worked up, but slightly raise my voice, "My surveyor says he measured everything again himself after the event, and there were no deviations in the marking. So, tell me, what the hell is going on here, then?"

"Listen, Eric," Rodriguez says with unease, this time remaining seated. "It's a pretty complex plan. There are three designers here, all of whom know their jobs, and all the drawings were authorized by your company, as well. Maybe we need to look elsewhere?"

I see where he's going with this and decide to nip it in the bud, "You're not blaming Kevin for this, Rodriguez. He follows the drawings to a T. You could just as well blame the excavator operator." I look over at Kevin, who nods his head slightly to show he appreciates my support. "I'm not talking about Kevin," Rodriguez quickly responds. "You know what we do when we have different elements designed by different designers on the same project, right?"

I do. And not just me. As if choreographed, everyone

turns their heads simultaneously to look at Janna Young, the design coordinator. She smiles with her arms folded over her chest, cool as a cucumber, wholly unbothered by the attention. "I was wondering when this was going to come," she snickers.

She pulls up a drawing of the "Disaster Area" on her gilded laptop, including in it the road, the wall supporting it, and the cable running parallel to them. In the center, a cartoon-like image of an explosion marks the site of the incident. "Look here," she says patronizingly, like she's lecturing freshmen students at engineering school, placing the cursor over the red line marking the high-voltage cable. "As you can see, there are six feet between the cable and the support wall – exactly two times what Mr. Harrison said they took as a precaution. The reason we doubled the distance is because we took into account the support wall's leg, which Mr. Harrison did not see in the main drawing which is viewed from above. When he looked at that drawing, all he could see was the head of the wall, from which he accordingly measured the distance," she points to the head of the wall in the plan. "We looked at this from a horizontal perspective, as well," she switches from the main drawing to another sketch, showing the cross section of the road, "and we could see that the wall's leg protrudes out three feet from the wall, which is why we took another three feet, to retain the safety distance."

Until that moment, I was sure they had simply forgotten about the leg, and that that's what caused this mess. In fact, I was waiting for everyone to finish speaking so I could show them their mistake. In one fell swoop, Ms. Young completely destroyed my argument.

"Are you serious?" Kevin steps in and angrily remarks, "Do you really not get that even if you marked six feet, when I excavate using heavy machinery, I need extra space to make that leg?"

"The leg might be just three feet away from the wall," he goes on, "but you need to cast the leg onto a layer of thin concrete, which is itself cast over foundation layers of sub-base in the ground. Each of these layers is broader than the one above it and, furthermore, the sides of the excavated ground are inclined, meaning the ditch gets wider and wider as you dig deeper. By the time you reach the depth of the cable, we'd have dug about eight feet away from the wall. In other words, you placed the cable right in the middle of the excavation for the wall. That's why the excavator hit it."

"I'm not the one who set your itinerary and determined the safety distances you require," Janna keeps her cool. "This is an execution problem, not a design problem. I mean, you don't expect me to advise you on handling excavators, right?"

She shuts her computer and starts to pack up her things, as if to say *I came, I saw, I conquered.* The young planners sit up in their chairs, preparing to hear closing words. Kevin looks at me with an irked, frustrated expression. I stand up and gesture for everyone to stay seated, "Listen. For the life of me, I don't understand how a serious group of individuals such as yourselves could spend an hour of their time reviewing this incident and all you come up with are arguments to prove that none of this was your responsibility. At the end of the day, we have a design problem here, and none of you – the design team – are willing to assume responsibility. You'd think I was sitting in front of a bunch of seasoned lawyers and PR strategists, not a group of talented engineers whose very profession is predicated on problem solving." I've been around this business long enough to know that in such cases it's every man for himself; I too am not here simply out of the kindness of my heart, but that doesn't make the situation any less frustrating. I look over at Bill Blackstone, who has been silent so far, and ask him, "Mr. Blackstone, you represent the DOT. This is your project, its success is your success, and everyone in this room is working for you. Can you assist us here?"

He slowly glances over at each of us, before eventually saying, "The DOT employs TWT Planning, the chief designer," he looks over at Rodriguez, "who oversees a team of consultants including you," he turns to Janna, Amy, and Harrison, "and employs the main contractor, Rhombus," he now points with his eyes at me and Kevin, "which oversees all the subcontractors of this project, including the one who tore the high-voltage cable. The reason we employ all of you is because we ourselves don't know how to design or execute such projects. That's your job. And yet, without even going deep, I can see at least four or five possible solutions here. If I were in any one of your shoes, let me reiterate– *every one of you*, I could offer a solution that would work in this situation. Now, because I am certain you are all no less talented than me, I assume you can see the options yourselves. But if I were to propose these solutions, I have no doubt that sooner or later one of you, if not all of you, would come to me and claim that I was the one who asked for this solution, so I should also be the one to pay for it. That is why I'm throwing the ball back to you. The problem here is not on the commissioner's side. It's either design or execution. Either the designers or the contractors need to work this out; ideally, it should be both of you."

In the pit of my stomach, I have the feeling that something's not right, but I can't put my finger on it. It looks like no one cares about this project. Not the various designers, not even the very one who commissioned the project and is paying for it. Or rather, it's not that they don't care, insomuch as it seems that each of them has a more pressing priority. As far as they're concerned, if they have to choose between the good of the project and covering their own asses, the answer's obvious. As long as they've got themselves covered, to hell with the project.

Now I'm not sure who I'm angrier with, him or them. "Okay everyone, we're done here," I wrap up the meeting. "Thanks for all your help."

## 4. THE SUBCONTRACTOR'S CONFLICT OF INTERESTS

When they say, "business meeting in a restaurant," they're definitely not talking about this place. I'm sitting at a shabby table in an old diner; a tired waitress is handing me a worn-out, stained plastic menu. Why am I here out of all the places in the world? Location.

I got Nick Waters to agree to meet me in the middle of a workday, a feat in and of itself. Since he signed with us to undertake the construction of the wall, we had only spoken over the phone, exchanging documents via email. As someone who took over for his father running the family firm, he doesn't believe in delegating authority—he's in charge of everything, from hiring employees, purchasing the machinery, right down to the branding of the company vehicles. Usually, when his company is working on a project he doesn't budge from the site, but after I emphasized how important it was for me to speak with him face-to-face, he agreed to meet me for a coffee at the gas station near the site he's working on. After all, a contract worth in excess of $1 million is no trifling matter for his company.

So, I'm waiting for him with a particularly bad cup of coffee on my table. You can ask for a refill, but I seriously doubt anyone would want to do that.

I sit facing the entrance, as I always do. I see him walking in. Waters doesn't just build walls, he looks like them as well; a giant of a man, dressed in a wide pair of jeans and a plaid flannel shirt, the sound of his work boots thunderously echo in the room as he stomps across the floor. They don't make 'em like that anymore.

"To what do I owe the pleasure, Mr. Price?" his powerful handshake nearly breaks my hand. His clothes smell of earth and dust.

"Hey Nick, thanks again for coming to meet me. What can I get you?"

"Nothing. Let's get straight to the point. I'm assuming you're here because of the incident you had with the high-voltage line, right?"

You can always count on rumors to spread fast in this business. "Right. So, you know what happened?"

"Yes, I know. The designers screwed you with a couple of months delay." I wish everyone agreed to this version of the story.

"Before we dive into the details, I wanted to run by you if we can make a slight change to your schedule."

"What kind of change?" he asks.

"Same wall, same materials, same measurements – only you do it in two segments. You see, we're going to have to move the cable again and that's going to take time. Instead of us sitting around doing nothing for a couple of months, you'll start putting up the part of the wall the cable doesn't interfere with. We'll move the cable in the meantime, and you complete the wall right after we're done. What do you think?"

"What do I think?" he asks a bit too loudly. "I think it'll cost you a lot of money and do you very little good."

I expected it to cost me, naturally, that's the way it is with subcontractors. I've never met one who agreed to making any change without being compensated, even if it doesn't cost him a thing. Like us, they also face fierce competition over projects with very little financial gain, so they have to profit from these changes in order to keep their heads above the water. But that it wouldn't be beneficial to me—that one took me by surprise.

"What's the problem doing it in two segments? You won't need to order any extra materials, and the equipment is the same."

"Look," he says to me as he gestures to the waitress, "you want a wall that's one thousand, three hundred feet long and thirteen feet tall, right?"

"Okay…?"

"We do the concrete in eight weeks. When that's done, we let it harden for three weeks, and then we need to fill in layers of soil behind it for four more weeks."

"Why so many?" I ask.

"If every layer we work on is eight inches thick, then we have twenty layers, right?"

"Okay…?"

"That's twenty layers, each of them needs to be spread, wetted, and compacted, then we have to wait till the next day for it to dry before we can place the next layer over it."

My next *okay* is a bit more hesitant.

"That means that the filling takes twenty workdays, which is four weeks. Doing the whole wall will take fifteen weeks," he sums up, "eight for the concrete, three for hardening, and four more for filling."

I skip the *okay*, but he goes on anyway, "If we split the

construction into two segments, then each half of the concrete work would take about a month – but waiting for the hardening and filling would take the same amount of time, meaning the second half of the wall wouldn't take half of fifteen weeks, but eleven weeks. All you'd be saving is four weeks."

"So, I'll save four weeks of work on the most crucial segment of the project and save myself a one million dollars delay penalty."

"Wow," he says. "I didn't realize these were the kind of sums we were talking about. In that case, maybe it is worth the effort, despite the extra charges."

"What extra charges? According to our contract, I'm paying you four hundred and eighty dollars per cubic meter of concrete. That includes the materials, earthwork, management, and overhead…" I pause for a second, "everything. There's no difference if you do it all in one shot or in two segments."

"If you keep saying that, you might end up believing it…" He pauses for a moment as the waitress sets down the beer he ordered. He doesn't bother pouring it into a glass, taking a long swig straight from the bottle. "If I split the work on the wall and start the second part only after I finish the first, then instead of paying for the engineer, the operation manager, and the trailer for fifteen weeks, I'll be paying for twenty-six weeks. I'm no math whiz, but even I know that's almost double."

I saw this coming. The overhead always increases when a job takes longer than expected. On the other hand, it pales in comparison to the monthly fine.

"Furthermore, I'll have to pay a lot more for my earth-moving equipment," he goes on.

Whoops. Didn't see that coming.

"Why's that?" I ask.

"Because in order to spread a filling layer along the wall and compact it, I need two trucks, a power shovel, a water tanker, a compactor, and a construction quality control manager to inspect and approve that each layer is sufficiently hardened before I can start work on the next one," he tells me, as if I were new to the profession. "This crew can lay a layer across the entire wall - one thousand, three hundred feet in one day, but even if I use the crew for only half of that length, I still need all of it. I can't give up a single worker or piece of equipment. The daily cost of this crew is about five thousand dollars and if we start the second half of the wall right after completing the first half, you'll have to pay for another eleven weeks. You do the math."

$250,000—no, $275,000.

I'm incensed by the audacity of him to suggest such an excessive figure. I feel the veins in my neck beginning to swell. The whole wall costs $1 million to put up, and to execute it in two segments, without adding a single drop of concrete, metal, or dirt he wants a 27 percent increase? Not on my watch.

"Nick," I remind him as gently as my anger permits me, "you signed a contract which, last time I read it, said that efficiency is your business. You work efficiently, you make a profit; you work inefficiently, you don't."

"Listen, Eric, I may look unsophisticated in these clothes, I don't wear a fancy tie and I don't throw around the fancy words lawyers do, but I know very well what the contract says. Everything we agreed to is predicated on us being able to work at full capacity. It doesn't say a single word about dividing the work or keeping my workers on standby for you to call on when you're ready. I'm amazed I even have to say this to you. You know that the price I offered is made up of costs, work, and our profit margin. If you change the conditions so that our costs go up, then obviously the price has to go up as well."

A silence pervaded the table when he finished talking, prompting him to erroneously assume I'm waiting for him to elaborate further. He then hits a soft spot. "I explained this to Silver as well, the guy who came up with your project's schedule. He came in with this idea of critical chain that supposedly was going to get you to finish this project on time. I showed him that the work breakdown his software produced was completely absurd, that it had me starting and stopping my own work midway five times to accommodate other subcontractors. No matter how many times I showed him that his breakdown would bring up my costs by causing such disruption, he insisted that it was the best solution for the project, because it cut execution time to a minimum."

Introducing critical chain project management into project 612 was my initiative from the very outset. I decided to go for it after taking a week-long course on the method, which convinced me this was the only way to deliver projects on time. Now this giant of a man comes along, and not only does he tell me that that goddam wall is going to cost me 27 percent extra, now he tells me Dr. Silver—the expert scheduler I brought in specially to make sure we deliver this project on time—doesn't know what he's doing? This is too much.

"But he really did cut the execution time to a minimum," I snap back. "He planned the shortest itinerary possible with the resources at our disposal." I want to get up and leave already, but then he says, "He may have cut the execution time down on paper. In reality—the project will take longer because of that stupid method."

I feel my heart racing and my palms sweating. Dr. Riley warned me that when I feel these symptoms I need to just stop and calm down, but how can I calm down now? "Where the hell do you get off saying such a thing?" I explode. "Where do you get the confidence from? Critical chain has been proven as the best method in the world to get projects done on time, and it's been just that for forty years!"

Talking to this human wall is about as effective as speaking to the walls he builds.

"It's very simple," he replies slowly. "I asked the other subcontractors on this project if their work breakdown created disruptions for them as well, and they all said yes. Ortega from electric even told me that that's part of the theory behind critical chain, and that according to this theory, the stops and starts and the idle time between them are deemed part of the solution, not the problem."

"That's right. Starts and stops are an inevitable part of the process," I respond. "Critical chain simply acknowledges that."

He looks at me with pity in his eyes. "Eric, you mean to tell me that you signed a contract with me where you drive my prices down to floor, based on me being able to work consistently and efficiently, and only after I sign it you bring this so-called-expert from the academy to tell me when I have to stop and when I have to start? Not only that, you then tell me I have to pay for it as well, because it's for the good of *your* project? You know, where I grew up, someone might call that a scam."

Deep inside, I have to admit that doesn't sound good, but I tell Nick, "If you're so smart, tell me how you solved it. If you're such an expert at making schedules—what did you do to finish on time?"

"Come on," he says without hesitation, "I did what we always do. I ignored the university kid and went ahead to build the wall in one shot, like I know how. I brought a full crew on to the site and they operate all day every day, without even looking at the schedule. When we finish doing everything we can, we move on to another project and work straight there as well. When we finish the other project, if you're ready to continue, we go back to your site. That's it."

"And if we're ready way before you're done with your other project?"

"Then you wait for us to finish," he delivers the final blow.

"But what if your work is on the project's critical chain? What if your delays hold back the entire project and costs us forty thousand dollars for each day we're late?"

"Listen," he says, pausing for a moment. "If I call the waitress over right now and order a burger and fries, demanding that it get here—hot and fresh—in exactly five minutes, you'd call that an unrealistic expectation, right?"

"Right, but what does that have to do with it?"

"Well, it's not unrealistic. McDonald's does it, for example.

But it means the entire kitchen staff has to keep that order on the grill at any given time, and that the restaurant has to be prepared to throw it away if no customer comes in to buy it when it's ready. If time is so valuable for you, perhaps what you need to do is pay us to sit there on your site ready to be called into action when you need us. The problem then would be that you couldn't buy our services at a rate of four hundred and eighty dollars per cubic meter, you'd have to add five thousand dollars for every day we shut-down operations—payment for time wasted."

With the 612 so far beneath the red line, paying extra for anything is not an option, so putting up the wall in two segments is off the table. But besides that, I get that feeling again in the bottom of my stomach that something is off. Really, really off. Not only is Nick Waters not about to solve my wall problem, he's telling me he's going to screw up the project's schedule even in places where there are no problems. Furthermore, he's telling me that all the other subcontractors on the project are doing the same thing. Finally, he's telling me that my secret weapon for dealing with schedule problems is fundamentally flawed.

"Tell me, Nick," I can't help but ask, even though I think I know what his answer is going to be, "you said before that you spoke about this with the other subcontractors who work on this project. Do you know how they're all dealing with the issue of working consistently?"

"It depends on their workload," he answers without pause, "those who have a lot of work throughout the project, such as the earthworks subcontractor, bring a permanent crew to the site and work the whole time. They don't take into account that your schedule requires occasionally shutting crews down and bringing in reinforcement crews at other times, because they know you're not going to pay—neither for the shut-down nor for the reinforcements. Instead, they schedule their crews so that they have their hands busy at all times, even if that means not following your critical path or critical chain or whatever. Other subcontractors, who only work on the project sporadically, move their crews on to other sites and when they finish there, they go back to yours. None of us subcontractors take your schedule too seriously, because we know you general contractors aren't going to pay for the stops and starts you cram into it. Furthermore, we all know that the main use of the schedule is to submit claims and change requests to the owner, for being the one responsible for the project's delays, and that's something between you general contractors and them, which has nothing to do with us subcontractors."

This is the second time during this conversation I feel the ground slipping from under my feet. Is he saying that everything I learned in the critical chain course is true only in theory? That Dr. Silver, the leading expert on critical chain project management in the Midwest (that's what his website says) was playing me for a fool? That for all intents and purposes, the schedule he made for the 612 exists only on paper, and that none of my subcontractors follow it?

I employ subcontractors to execute every aspect of this project, so if Waters is right…

## 5. THE DESIGNER AND OWNER'S OWN CON-FLICTS OF INTEREST

Danielle's tailored attire, with a finely pressed dress shirt beneath a sharp black blazer, probably impresses those who don't know any better—but I notice she sloppily misbuttoned her shirt, and recall the shenanigans she and I used to pull as kids.

"Hey, brother," she says, without a hug or kiss, a blend of familial affability and professional correctness.

"Hello, Danielle," I adopt the distant tone she sets.

She sits at her desk, turns her eyes away from the two large computer screens, and slightly moves the glass mug with a slice of lemon in front of her. "Rodriguez tells me the meeting wasn't very productive." That's quite an understatement. "Tell me what happened."

I realize this is not going to be a friendly chat between siblings, so I get straight to the point. "What happened was that your people came to my site and all they did was pass the blame from one to the other, until finally deciding that I should be held accountable for this goddamned drawing, which, by the way, I saw for the first time only after the cable had already been moved. They didn't even care what the problem was, they just wanted to make it clear that they had nothing to do with it."

"Okay, Eric, first of all, they're not 'my people;' they are subcontractors' consultants, the same way as how most of those you employ are not your own employees but subcontractors."

"Oh, give me a break," I cut her off, but she doesn't seem to be bothered.

"Come on, Eric, you're not a child. You know I need to protect my office the same way you need to protect your company." We both know she's right, but to hear that from my little sister stings. "And besides, did you really expect them to come up with a solution?" As a matter of fact, I did, but once Danielle frames the question like that, I choose to just let it slide.

"Danielle, you're lead design for this project; it means as much to you as it does to me, right?"

"Supposedly."

I see this isn't going to go any smoother than yesterday's meeting.

"You know what?" I try a different approach, "forget about our positions. If I were to tell you over dinner that I had a problem with a miss located high-voltage cable, never mind whose fault it was—what would you suggest I do?"

She stalls. First, she insists she wouldn't talk business at the dinner table. Then, she says it depends on the particular context and circumstances, and, only after I corner her, she finally offers a solution. "Well, if you put it that way, I would suggest not bothering with moving the high-voltage cable again, but simply changing the type of wall."

Finally, we're making progress. "What did you have in mind? A reinforced soil wall?"

"Exactly."

I've used this method several times before; it's quite simple. Instead of casting a leg—a tall concrete wall requiring a space-consuming broad concrete foundation—you cast a narrow foundation, over which you place a row of concrete blocks, each fitted with metal braces at the bottom. The braces are tightened on one side of the concrete blocks and are covered with a layer of packed soil. The weight of the soil keeps the braces in place, which in turn fix the concrete blocks in place and prevent the soil mass from moving them. You then build another row of blocks on top and repeat the process as many times as necessary. That way, you don't need a broad concrete leg like with a cast concrete wall, so we'd gain that 3 ft. of space and wouldn't have to move the high-voltage cable again.

"Okay, Danielle. How long would it take you to design such a thing?" I ask, giving her a look that says *spare me the negotiation*. She gestures that she understands, checks something in her computer, looks up at me and says, "I believe we can have a plan ready in two weeks' time."

Two weeks. Even without calculating the cost of each day wasted times two weeks, I can see that there's a lot of money on the line here. On the other hand, two weeks is a reasonable time, and if she keeps it (Danielle always meets her deadlines), we could look at this whole thing as nothing more than a minor blip along the way.

"Fine, you sold me on it," I say and smile at her as if we were fighting over the remote in our parents' living room. "Can you start right away?"

It seems like something softens in her expression, and I see my little sister again instead of a hardened business rival. "Sure," she says, and smiles back at me. "I just need one thing from you."

"Whatever you need," I feel overcome with generosity.

"I need you to get me a work order from the DOT."

"What did you say?" Where the hell did that come from? The cordial atmosphere dissipates instantly.

"Why are you so surprised? Without a work order, I am effectively assuming responsibility over the incident. Do you think our legal consultant would ever agree to such a thing?"

Siblings or not, this is really pushing my buttons. "Tell me, do you even know what this means?" I ask in the tone of an older brother reprimanding his annoying little sister.

"Of course I do. It means you get a work order, and two weeks later you can put up the wall. If that doesn't suit you, by all means, follow the usual protocol. You'll send me a request for information asking for a solution to the cable's current location, and I'll forward it to the DOT, who will forward it to the electric company, who'll blow a fuse when they realize they're being asked to relocate a cable they just moved less than two years ago. In the end, the DOT will get a work order for the relocation of the cable, and you won't be able to resume work until the electric company moves the cable. It'll take a month for the DOT to issue a work order, three more months for the electric company to design a plan for the relocation, and another three months for them to execute the plan."

"You're evading the question—how do you reconcile the fact that all of this mess comes from your department, with me having to go to the DOT and get you a work order? The electrical designer works for you, the wall designer works for you, the systems coordinator works for you, and all of you together managed to botch up the cable relocation. If I were you, I'd get five people to sit down and get new drawings ready before the weekend. Otherwise, the DOT will have your heads."

"Eric, you need to separate the facts on the ground from the rules of the game," she answers, composed and unbothered by my rant. "On our end, I've already called those three idiots in for a briefing, and I'll try to draw conclusions from this to avoid it happening again in the future. But as the rules of the game between us, yourselves, and the DOT are concerned, that's a whole other ball game. Design-wise, not only is the original plan we proposed a valid and suitable solution for the circumstances of the road, it's also the cheapest solution. No one **expressly asked for a temporary solution** for the high-voltage line for the construction period…" she pauses and reiterates her point for emphasis, "No one **expressly asked us** for a temporary solution. And that's exactly what I'll say to the DOT when they ask me why I didn't move the cable farther."

"The alternative you ask," she continues, "that I call the authority to say that we dropped the ball and that we'd like to correct our error would force them to sue us over our insurance policy, otherwise they'd have to risk an internal inquiry suggesting they preferred our office over another whose insurance policy they did sue over. If they do sue over our insurance policy, we'll have to defend ourselves, and we'll say that…" she pauses and lets me finish, "That no one expressly asked you for a temporary solution."

"That's right," she replies as if she were a grade-school teacher and I the dweeb who raised his hand and gave the correct answer.

"That would inevitably lead to the DOT having to take responsibility for not issuing a work order for the construction period—and they're never going to do that. They're fully aware of what would happen if they did; they were in the same situation last year with Bedford & Sons. You remember that in the end it was their engineer who oversaw the project—one of the best I ever worked with—who took responsibility for what happened, and he was promptly fired. They don't want a repeat of that. So, a solution for which they take the blame is out of the question."

She can see that this backward logic is a pill I'm having a hard time swallowing, so she softens her tone, "Put yourself in their position. Nobody's own money on the line. Public sector wages. Slow promotions, and legal advisers whose main objective is to avoid losing in court. You wouldn't want to risk a lawsuit which could see you end up getting pinned with the blame, either." She's right again. I can't tell if she's really trying to protect me, or if this is just a rhetorical trick.

"The bottom line is that as far as the DOT is concerned, there is no simple solution. Therefore, it would take months for them to issue us a work order to relocate the cable. What I'm suggesting you do is get me a work order, as soon as tomorrow, to change the wall, not the cable; that'll cut down your delay by six months. Plus, it'll allow you to bill them for the expensive rather than the cheap wall. In other words, this is the best solution for me, for you, and for the DOT," she concludes and looks me in the eye.

What I find most stunning about this crazy conversation is the role reversal, my little sister explaining to me how the world works, while I, her older brother, the one who's always told her what she needs to do and where she's wrong, stands there dumbfounded without a single intelligent thing to say in response.

"Say, how're the kids?" she asks after we finish the business side of this meeting. *So now you're my sister again?* I think to myself, irked.

"You know... Fine. I think they're about to have a little less daddy time in the near future."

"Well, if you need a hand, you know where to reach me, right? Let's try to get together before Josh's birthday, okay?"

"When's that?" I ask, a little embarrassed my sister knows better than me when my own kid's birthday is.

"Beginning of next month. Karen's probably planning something nice. Remember, you promised them two parties every year, right?"

Right. That's what I need now—a party.

# 6. CONFLICTS OF INTEREST BETWEEN A PLAYER AND HIS TEAM

It's a 25-minute drive from our house to Greenfield High School and, over the past two years, I've memorized the way over. Since Ashley and Jayden met, I can't even remember where, my daughter has become a basketball fan. Well, not a basketball fan per se, more like one particular basketball player's fan; but give her a whiteboard and a marker, and she'll run you through Greenfield's entire offensive playbook, and explain why boxing out to get your rebound is the most important team play. Where was she all those years I spent watching ESPN alone? We go to all of Greenfield's home games together, and big games, such as the one today, the boys tag along. Even Karen occasionally comes. Actually, there hasn't been a game as important as the one we're going to today. St. Thomas, our direct rivals (how did it already become "our"?) are ranked top ten in the state, thanks to James Tig, the most talked about high school player in the country. That means today will be a festive day at Greenfield, the national press will be there, scouts from all the top colleges will be in the stands, and the stands will be packed to the rafters. Jayden, being Greenfield's star player, always gets tickets to the best seats in the house, and this time Ashley asked him for five. You don't need to be a basketball expert to understand just how important this game is to Jayden. A good performance will likely score him a great scholarship at a good college, boosting his chances of making it to the NBA and possibly making him set for life. On the other hand, a poor performance would suggest to the scouts that he can't handle the pressure, and perhaps isn't suited to the big leagues.

Even though as a kid I dreamed of being a professional athlete, truth is, I don't envy Jayden. I have a lot of pressure riding on me at my job, but at least no one broadcasts it on TV. And besides, I know that if worse comes to worst, there'll always be another project.

The ride over to Greenfield always flies by. Usually, Ashley and I get some quality time together while the boys fool around in the back, and we stop for ice cream or burgers on the way. But this time, it's different—Ashley's silent almost the entire ride over, nervously twitching her legs and occasionally asking me if we'll get there on time. I'm not too communicative either, my thoughts have a life of their own and keep taking me back to that torn cable, the tumultuous meeting at Danielle's office, and the inevitable meeting with the clients at the DOT. The boys are quiet in the back as well, they can sense something is different about today.

"Go Tigers!" I shout when the car pulls into the parking lot and we prepare to head toward the stadium, but no one replies with the famous Greenfield roar.

Ashley gets the envelope with our tickets, and we pile in. You can feel the special atmosphere, the stands are almost completely full, and everyone's taking pictures. If you're not holding a cell phone camera, you're holding a TV camera. The players from both teams, still in their track suits, are warming up on the court.

"Ashley, why aren't we in our regular seats?" Ben asks

after we sit down. He's right, we usually have courtside seats, so close to the action you can see the ribbed texture of the orange basketball. But this time, we're in the eighth row, slightly over to the side. "Think," she snaps at him, and Karen immediately tosses me a look telling me not to reprimand her. "Sweetie," she softly says to Ben, "there are a lot of important people coming to the game today, and they are official guests of Greenfield." We've been living apart for three years now, but the dynamics of how we handle the kids haven't changed. "Besides," Josh jumps in, "these seats are much better."

"No they're not!" Ben is unconvinced. "Everyone knows courtside seats are the most expensive." Well, they are, but it seems the younger brother is right this time, sitting courtside means you're close to the action, but when you go up a couple of rows, you suddenly get a panoramic view of the court. I already get a different sense of the court's proportions and see more players in action, including James Tig—who so far during warm-up hasn't missed a single shot. He looks the real deal.

Meanwhile, Ashely goes down to the first row to have her ceremonial pre-game kiss with Jayden. They do this before every game, and I still feel a bit uncomfortable watching them kiss in front of everyone (especially, if I'm being honest, in front of me).

When the game starts, with all due respect to the fact that there are ten people running around the court and two sweaty coaches and their teams on the sidelines, this is a two-man show, James Tig and Jayden Green are playing like this was a one-on-one game in their backyard.

A person in a tiger suit keeps waving at the crowd to get it pumped up, a group of cheerleaders in uniform that is both too short and too tight is dancing during timeouts, and the announcer has all but spent his voice in the first half alone. Everyone seems to be having a great time besides Ashely, who is sitting on the edge of her seat nervously biting her fingernails.

Tig demonstrates exactly why the press follows him everywhere, and Jayden can't keep up with him and starts missing shots. As St. Thomas' lead slowly gets into double digits, the crowd begins to realize this is not going to be like all the other home games this season.

Karen sits next to Ashley, maintaining a reasonable distance between us, while I in turn sit between the boys, occasionally commentating on the plays, turning their attention to defensive plays and things going on off court. "If you really want to get this game," I say to Ben and Josh but also to Karen and Ashley, "don't watch the ball." Often times, the drama is on the other side of the play, a movement to the other side of the court, a block on the shooting guard, or a drive into the center that opens up a pass to the point guard. Basketball commentators call that *the stuff you don't see in statistics*.

I occasionally glance at my cell phone, waiting to get approval from the office for the meeting on Tuesday with Martin Chambers of the DOT, until I remember that we're actually deep into the weekend and no one but me is thinking about this meeting now. Well, no one but me and Danielle.

"Why does Jayden shoot the ball in every attack?" Josh suddenly asks. I nervously glance over at Ashley, but she didn't hear his question. "What do you mean? Because he's the best player, stupid," Ben answers his younger brother, as gentle as ever... "But he keeps missing," Josh insists, and he's right again. Ashley now picks up on the conversation. "Don't you realize every newspaper in the country is going to be writing about this game? You think he can afford to end with just six points?"

"But the most important thing is that the Tigers win, isn't it?" Karen and I look at Josh with a mix of surprise and pride. We raised a fine kid.

"The most important thing is that next year we can go to Connecticut, or Marquette, or North Carolina," Ashley says. Karen and I lock eyes and share a moment of apprehension; we can live with a seven-mile commute, but flying out nine hundred and thirty miles every time we want to see our daughter is a different matter altogether.

"Dad, it doesn't matter who wins, then?" Josh throws the question over to me.

"Of course the most important thing is that the Tigers win, Josh. Basketball is a team sport, and these types of games are only won with a group effort," I say what a dad is expected to say, but I don't really believe my own words. "In this specific case, it's important that Jayden scores a lot of points, because we want him to keep progressing and maybe one day play professionally." Karen signals that I did good, but Josh isn't satisfied, "But you said you can be good without scoring, by doing all that statistics stuff."

"The things you *don't* see in statistics," Ben corrects him and looks over to me, waiting to hear my response.

"You're right, kids. But think about it this way, if the coach of an important college team is watching from the stands, out of all the players, who does he notice?"

"James Tig!" Josh yells out. Ashley throws him a *I'm gonna kill you* look.

"I mean, what kind of player is always considered the best?"

"Oh, that's easy," Ben replies, "the one who scores the most."

"And that's why Jayden shoots all the time, even though he misses most of them?" I look over to Ashley again, but she's not listening to the conversation anymore. I'm not sure what to tell Josh, who understands perfectly what's going on. The more Jayden takes the game upon himself, the less chances Greenfield has of winning the game. But if I were him, what would I prefer, a chance to win the game with my high school team, or a chance to land a lucrative college scholarship?

The answer's obvious.

At halftime, I look at Mr. O'Reilly, Greenfield's coach, and ask myself why he is okay with what's going on? You don't need a coach to let Jayden shoot every time in the hope that he scores (or—on the rare occasion—passes), even the tiger mascot can do that. But maybe the coach is also part of this broader game, in which his team can't possibly win the national championship, but can become a breeding ground for future pros. Does Mr. O'Reilly prefer to be the guy who used to coach NBA-star Jayden Green, or the guy who led Greenfield High School to the regional quarter-finals? Either way, St. Thomas take an easy sixteen-point lead, and their coach gives Tig—who has already accumulated three fouls—a rest, prompting Mr. O'Reilly to seize the opportunity to give Jayden a rest as well. Jayden sits down on the bench and buries his face in his towel, hardly looking up at his teammates on the court. He doesn't even hear Ashley, who has left her seat and gone down to the second row, trying to shout encouraging words to her disheartened star.

Jayden's teammates seem to do all right without him and manage to cut St. Thomas' lead to just six points with 90 seconds to go in the first half. Their coach quickly sends Tig back in to protect their lead, and O'Reilly reciprocates by recalling Jayden. I look down at him from the stands, my daughter's boyfriend, and I kind of feel sorry for him, he's the only one who can in any way measure up to Tig, making his responsibilities, both offensive and defensive, a lot harder than those of his teammates. But if he wants to make it to the NBA, then he should be able to thrive in adversity, shouldn't he?

Then suddenly it happens, Jayden blocks Tig's shot, getting the crowd riled up, and plows down the court in a counterattack. The boys are on their feet. Jayden's team are two-on-one, so Jayden just has to pick the right pass and the Tigers get an easy two points. But Jayden's not looking for easy points and, bolstered by the rapturous crowd, he soars up to the hoop to dunk the ball. The defender realizes the show is going to be at his expense and stops him mid-air with an ugly foul. Jayden lands awkwardly on his ankle, and despite the crowd's loud cheering, the whole stadium hears him scream in pain. That includes Ashley, who runs toward the court until she is stopped by an usher in the first row. She turns to look up at us; I can see tears and a look of horror in her eyes. This can't be happening to us now.

## 7. EVEN THE OWNER ANSWERS TO SOMEONE, WITH THEIR OWN CONFLICTS OF INTEREST

I've met Martin Chambers—manager of the DOT, and the person who called Danielle and me to this special meeting—several times over the years. The last time was in a job interview four months ago that somehow came to nothing. But this time it's a completely different matter; this time, it's not about me becoming the new chief engineer of the DOT, but about the complaints I have as the contractor's representative against the DOT, so this meeting is not going to be as cordial.

Turning right off the highway takes me to a large lot that at one time was probably an open field, but today houses the DOT building—an unimpressive four-story office building, with a tidy lawn out front and a busy parking lot packed with SUVs.

I immediately spot Danielle's yellow Alpha-Romeo. I knew she'd be early.

"Hello, Mr. Chambers," I confidently say after his secretary leads me into the office where we held the job interview a few months back. "I see you've already met my sister."

Chambers looks comfortable sitting in an executive chair behind his desk. It's the end of the day, but he looks as fresh and neat as if it had just begun.

"That I did, and I'm impressed. But please, call me Martin. We are close enough acquaintances for you to allow yourself to be late, aren't we?"

"Oh, sorry about that," I see Danielle moving

uncomfortably in her seat. "Traffic, you know how it is."

"I do. And if you don't get moving with the 612, it's not going to get any easier to drive over here."

Touché.

Bill Blackstone, the fourth person in the room, waves hello at me.

"Okay, Eric, let's begin. Every time we hold an unscheduled meeting with project managers, I know there's trouble. Danielle has already brought me up to speed."

I look over at Danielle who buries her face in the paperwork she brought with her. What did she say already?

I begin to tell him all about the design and the approvals, our progress in the field, and how our entire company is throwing their backs into this project. I describe the meeting we held with the designers right after the incident, and my meeting with Danielle a couple of days ago. Chambers darts his eyes back and forth between me and Danielle, occasionally running his fingers through his silvery hair.

"That's slightly different from how your sister views it, but I think we get the picture."

"Slightly different?" I look over at Danielle with incredulous irritation. "Different how? Did I say anything that's not solid fact?"

"It seems your sister thinks so. Don't you, Ms. Price?" he seems to be relishing this.

"Not completely different," Danielle tries to diffuse the atmosphere, "but you can't portray this like the whole problem is down to the design. I sent Mr. Chambers the drawings this morning, and I think he agrees with me that's not where the problem was."

I can't believe she's doing this to me again.

"Then where was the problem? The excavator's bucket, perhaps? Or maybe the high-voltage cable simply snuck into our work zone the night before and forgot to inform you?!" I sense I'm starting to raise my voice, and try to calm down.

Danielle starts to answer, but Chambers intervenes. "Now, now, let's not get all worked up." He presses the intercom button on his desk and asks his secretary to bring in two large glasses of water. He looks at the two of us and says, "I can't imagine what a family dinner at your house must look like."

"Listen to me, both of you," he goes on. "This is not the first time I've run into a mess like this, and probably not the last. If you two want to keep playing the blame game, do it at your parents' house," he really loves this family gag. "In my office, we solve problems. We're the ones who commissioned this project, we're the ones who pay for it, and we're the ones who're going to have to answer to the governor and the media when they come knocking on our office door if this project keeps stalling. Got it? Now—solutions, please."

We both nod our heads.

I start to tell him about the reinforced soil wall, presenting the plan for how it would look, and Danielle adds the technical details. We actually make a very convincing team. We complete each other's points, each bringing their own strengths to the discussion, as if we had rehearsed this presentation for weeks rather than ad-libbing it.

"See, you might grow to like each other," Chamber signals he's pleased with this direction, "you might even be able to celebrate Christmas together."

"Okay, Price family," his voice becomes serious again, "let's talk business. I ask you plain and simple, so spare me the negotiations, how long and how much?"

After I run through the calculation of the added work and extra materials, Danielle adds the planning time (this time, she fully commits to two weeks) and cost. He nods along and types something into the computer in the corner of his desk. "You realize that every dollar you add to the bill comes directly from public funds, yes?"

We both nod along, though I don't really get where he's going with this. For all we care, he could just as well get the money from his grandmother, or from a casino in Las Vegas.

"Let me explain to you how things work in the government world. You see this?" he opens one of the drawers of his desk. "I don't have two hundred thousand dollars just lying around here. I would need a whole host of approvals to get my hands on that money."

"But you run this place," Danielle intervenes.

"Ms. Price. What do you do when you need to increase your budget? You go to your boss, right?"

She nods in approval.

"Well, it's the same for me. Only in my case, there are several bosses, each with their own agenda, and getting them all in the same room together takes two months. But suppose we manage to do that—after all, like you said, I run this place so I do hold some sway around here—what would this new wall you're proposing look like?"

"What do you mean?" I take the reins before Danielle starts lecturing him. "A concrete wall as high as it says in the drawings."

"You don't understand what I'm saying, my friend. I didn't ask about its measurements, I asked what it's going to look like. What would the cows grazing on the grass beneath it see?"

"Eric, let me take this. Mr. Chambers, we haven't reached that stage of the plan yet, but you'll be able to choose out of several options. It won't be a problem."

"Of course it's going to be a problem," he quickly retorts. "Every little change requires the approval of the committee. Ten people are gonna sit on that committee, and each of them is going to have something to say about it. In the end, we'll get to a point where the environmentalists lecture me on why this change critically upsets the balance of nature, or something like that. Believe me, I've been there many times before."

"I see what you're saying, sir. And I can guarantee you that in two-to-three days' time I'll have several options for the wall ready for the committee to review, and I'll personally see to it that everyone's happy, okay?"

Two-to-three days? Chamber just stares at her, not knowing where to start. "Ms. Price, this committee convenes once every two months, and even that is assuming that date doesn't happen to fall on a holiday or something. And considering the last time the committee convened was at the start of this week, you calculate yourself when the next meeting will be."

Danielle is flushed with embarrassment. For the first time, I can see that she realizes she still has some learning to do.

"And besides, if you were to come in with your plan and everyone were to approve it that same day—that would be an absolute miracle. I bet you a hundred dollars that someone is going to ask you for another design, or just decide they need some time to think about it, and just like that, another two months go by. I remind you; time is your enemy. I'm sure Eric is aware of the financial repercussions of each month you're late, right?"

I am.

"I'll help you out with the budget," he brings the conversation to a close, "but getting the committee to approve the plan is on you."

***

After three times I bug him on call waiting, Ethan finally calls me back.

"Well, how did it go with Chambers?"

I recount with as much detail as I can what we settled on in the meeting. He keeps silent the whole time, even after I finish. "Ethan, are you with me?"

"Yes, yes. Let's run through those numbers," he pauses again to get everything down. "We're looking at two weeks for design and another six weeks to get the committee's approval, and that's assuming there are no problems along the way, right?"

"Right."

"So, a two-month delay on the critical chain."

"Yes," I say and quickly qualify that conclusion again, "if everything is on time." As we've come to know, that's a stipulation that often doesn't materialize.

"So let's add that to the four-month delay from Thompson's time, and we're already six months off the deadline with a one percent fine for each month's delay."

I don't need a calculator to add those numbers up. "That's six million dollars, Ethan."

"And what about our overhead? If I'm being very liberal here, I add three million dollars in overhead, bringing us to nine million dollars. Remember how much our projected profit was when we bid for this project?"

"One and a half million."

He goes silent again, and this time—so do I. This hole we've dug ourselves into starts to take shape, and looking down, the floor seems to slip farther and farther away.

"How much credit do we have left with the bank?" I ask, even though I think I know the number. "Just under three million," Ethan confirms.

In other words—our heads are deep below the water.

"Ethan, has anyone looked over our contract lately? Is it possible we won't have to pay the whole six million?"

"I'm not sure that's the right question. As things stand, we really aren't at fault here, and I think we have a good shot at convincing a judge to agree, should it come to that. The problem is the time it would take us to prove we are not accountable for the delay. If we keep working and filling invoices by the book, we'll be past the date of our contractual obligation six months before we actually finish the project. Chambers might wait for a month or so, but after that he'll start withholding payments, because his lawyers will instruct him to deduct our late fees from our payments. That means we're not going to see those six million dollars before a court ruling, which would take about two years. At that point, even if the judge rules in our favor, it'll be two years too late. We'll be deep into bankruptcy by then."

"Ethan," I say after a long pause, "I'm sorry, but I'm out of ideas. Can you think of anything better than the alternative we offered?"

"No, but I can think of a better way of doing it."

I have no clue what he means. "A better way? Are you sure?"

"Maybe not better, but faster."

"Ethan, maybe I didn't explain the schedule clearly—"

"No, no. You explained just fine. But we have to cut it shorter. Listen, we can't wait for approvals. We have to start working right away."

"That's taking a crazy risk, Ethan." I couldn't have imagined that the pressure would drive him to make such an irrational decision. "What do we do if the committee doesn't approve? We just take down the wall?"

"I don't want to even think about that. The problem is the alternative is much worse. In fact, there is no alternative."

"So, how do you want to go about it?"

"First, talk to your sister. Have her start working on the drawings and tell her to get it over to us in steps—foundations and location first. We'll talk about cover later. Once I hang up with you, I'm calling Mark at Reinforced Walls. He's an expert in these types of walls. If we're lucky, he'll be available to start working in a couple of days."

"Okay. You do realize that Danielle will probably demand a financial commitment."

"Then commit," he answers concisely.

"Okay," I say. "I'll see you in the morning."

"Hold on, I'm not done with you yet."

What else does he want? I'll speak with Danielle and prepare Kevin for the possibility we're going to have to cut everyone's vacation short.

"I'm sending you Victor North's number. He's a landscape architect who represents the environmentalists on the DOT's committees. He's a good guy."

"What am I supposed to do with it?"

"I want you to meet him and come to an understanding about the wall. I can't have them putting a spoke in our wheel because some jackal wandering around at night might be scared of the metal braces or some other nonsense they might come up with."

"Are we allowed to do that?"

"Eric, we're past the point of working by the book. You're not calling him into your office, as far as I'm concerned you can run into each other at the store or at the movies. No protocol, no schedules, but reach an agreement."

I've never been asked to do such a thing before, and, honestly, I'm not too excited about it. "Ethan," I ask carefully, "is that legal?"

"Eric, I'm not sending you over with a bag of cash, you're not bribing anyone and you're not threatening anyone. North understands how this business works, he'll set us back years on this project if he thinks there's a problem. But if he doesn't, which I don't think he will, he'll realize it's best to streamline this thing."

That's a fair explanation, but I'm still having a hard time accepting it. I silently think to myself how I'm going to approach North over this.

"Eric, you got it?"

"Yeah, I got it."

"Good, then we both have work to do. Start with your sister, and we'll talk tomorrow at the office. Okay?"

## 8. THE ENVIRONMENTALISTS' INTERESTS

5:30 p.m. is a relatively quiet hour at Tom's Café. It's a little too late for business meetings, and a little too early for evening dates, so employees have an hour to leisurely prepare the next shift. Ashley brings me a large coffee and a fairly decent blueberry muffin. She even has a couple of minutes to sit and chat with me. She tells me about Jayden, and how his foot is slowly healing, about her studies, and even her plans for the future—which seem to change about every two weeks.

"I've been thinking about it, Dad. I think I want to be an economist," she says in full earnestness. "Economics is the most interesting class I have."

She notices a smirk on my face and is a little disappointed I don't share her enthusiasm.

"Sweetie, you've already told me you wanted to be an architect, a psychologist, a café owner, and… something else. I forgot. And that's only this past year."

"But this time it's different! I've been reading books outside of the syllabus, would you believe it?" Ashley's reading books without being forced to? That really is something.

"Forget about that, though. Who are you meeting this time?"

"Someone called Dr. Sally Erikson. She represents the environmentalist organizations on the general planning committee of the DOT."

"Who is she?"

"Actually, we've never met. I was supposed to meet her boss, but he's out of town. I was informed yesterday that I'll be meeting her instead of him. Anyway, she could be real trouble. One wrong word from her could set us back weeks, even months with the committee."

"So, you're trying to see what she plans to say to the committee?"

"More than that, Ashley. I'm going to try to reach an agreement with her about what she is going to say to the committee. Meaning, we reach a deal about the new design for the wall now and nip that potential bureaucratic mess in the bud. You understand?"

"What will she get in return for saving you all that money by saving you time?"

"Why should she get anything? All we're doing is moving things along. This way, the foxes and jackals get their wall ahead of schedule," I answer.

"And is that why you're meeting her here, at Tom's, rather than in your office?"

"That too. I see you pick up on things fast."

"What do you mean *that too*? What other reason do you have to be here?"

"Well, perhaps you don't pick up on things that fast, after all," I smile to her. "Here I can spend some time with my daughter." I sneak a peck on her cheek, and she quickly pulls back, embarrassed someone will see.

"I have to go anyway, Dad. There are tables that need service."

I did my homework last night on Facebook and Google ahead of this meeting. It turns out that Dr. Erikson is a lecturer in landscape architecture, a member of all sorts of activist and environmentalist foundations and institutions, and a marathon runner. Alongside the many articles she shares on her profile, most of which deal with sustainable design and stories about environmental disasters from around the world, there are quite a few pictures of her there, a selfie with her students, traveling with her two kids, and running marathons around the world. In every one of those pictures she is tall, red-headed, with kind and cheerful blue eyes. In short—stunning.

I didn't notice she'd come up to my table. "Mr. Price, I presume?" she asks, testing to see if I get the reference to Dr. Livingstone's meeting with Sir Henry Morton Stanley, when the latter found him in Africa.

"Hello Dr. Erikson," I stand. "Thank you so much for agreeing to meet with me. I would reply the same as Dr. Livingstone did, if only I could remember what it was that he said."

With black pants and a pearl-colored sweater, she looks just like her photos. My eyes linger on her just slightly too long.

"First of all, it's Sally. Second, I have practice tonight, so please, explain to me if what we're doing here is what I think it is."

She's not going to make this easy for me. "What do you mean?" I play innocent.

"You have a project that's going to be presented before the committee, and you want to close a deal with me in advance, so we won't hold you back. Am I right?"

I see there's no playing games with her, so I lay my cards

out on the table. "You're right."

"I can't say I'm pleased about it, but, believe it or not, we don't like bureaucracy either. What exactly is the problem?"

Ashley comes up to the table and turns to Sally, "What can I get you, ma'am?" She glances over at me and raises her eyebrows to show she is impressed. "This gentleman's paying, so you can have whatever you'd like."

Sally looked at her in confusion. "This is my daughter, Ashley," I step in to explain, "she still needs to learn some manners, but she's a great waitress."

She orders a carrot juice, and when Ashley walks away, Sally says, "I see you brought me to your home turf."

"Well, you know," I try to butter her up, "that's what you do when you play against a strong opponent."

I tell her about the new wall, the high-voltage cable, the meetings, and the approvals. She listens intently. I keep expecting her to interrupt me and protest about how we'd be hurting some rare frogs or destroying the natural habitat of a species of ants, or some other quirky thing. But she lets me finish presenting my case.

"Eric, Rhombus' problems are not my problems, so I don't really care how you intend to go about your business. Our authority lies only with protecting the environment. Please, explain to me what this new wall that you want us to approve is going to look like."

"Pretty simple, a concrete wall. You know."

"Smooth concrete, like in the designs you presented?"

I don't really get where she's going with this. "You know, concrete. Gray. In this case, it would be a square pattern, because that's how reinforced soil walls are built. That's it."

"Meaning, the change in plans affects the aesthetics of the wall, as well. Correct?"

"Yes. But at the end of the day, it's just concrete that supports a road. People who fly by it at sixty miles per hour don't even see it. We're not building a wall for the jackals and foxes to find pleasing."

Sally claps her hands together in irritation. "Every time environmental considerations come up, it's always the same tune—*who cares,* right?"

"I didn't say that, Sally," I quickly retreat. "We'll make it look however you want us to make it look." What I really want to say, but don't, is, *You guys would set us back for three months simply because of how a wall looks? People could lose their jobs over this!*

"Here's your juice, Dr. Erikson." Ashley places a tall orange glass before Sally and throws me another look. "Is everything okay?"

"You know, Ashley," Sally says, "your father and I are in the middle of a debate. Why don't you help us settle the matter?"

Ashley glances over at me apprehensively, but at this stage I think she could only do us good. I nod in approval.

"Good. Do you know what support walls on the side of highways look like?"

"Sure," Ashley answers quickly. "My dad always points out such elements when we're driving together." Her answer makes me proud, but I'm still suspicious about where Erikson is going with this.

"Do you know those walls covered with stones that look like they were built from locally-sourced material?"

"Yeah, I think I know what you mean. I think I recall my

dad telling me that's called stone cladding. Right?"

Sally turns to face me now, "I see your daughter is well versed in your field." I nod, failing to conceal a proud smile. "So, tell me Ashley, which do you think looks nicer—a stone clad wall, or a square-patterned gray concrete wall?"

Ashley realizes she's walked into a trap. She glances at me to get my approval. "Don't be shy, Ashley," I say, knowing what's about to happen. "Say what you think."

"I think a stone wall looks nicer," she says, and Sally smiles. "But it's more expensive, isn't it?"

"That's for your father to tell us."

"Ladies," I jump in, "I don't think you need me here for this negotiation. But just know that stone cladding like that costs about half a million dollars." I try not to overdo my exaggeration.

"I think your father is exaggerating a bit, dear," Erikson concludes, "but I've got an offer for him."

"I'm listening."

"How much would it cost you to make the wall from stone like stamped concrete?"

I run the numbers in my head and double the figure I arrive at. "About one hundred and eighty thousand dollars," I declare.

"So, what do you say, Price family—can we conclude this meeting with me getting another carrot juice from the daughter and a stamped concrete wall from the father? Tip's on me, anyway."

I look straight into her eyes and speak slowly, emphasizing every word, "You're taking advantage of the fact that we have to find a solution to a problem we weren't accountable for in the first place. If I didn't need your consent, I'd call that extortion."

I know I'm provoking her here, but she's unfazed, and answers quickly, "You're not the only one with constraints here. If I tell the people who sent me here that I met a contractor in dire straits and didn't take advantage of his distress to score even a small concession for the landscape and the environment, they'll be asking themselves if I'm the right person for the job."

How did I not see this coming? She can't make purely professional decisions, either. She has her own interests to protect.

I can see in Ashley's eyes a plea to bring this showdown to an end. She wants to be an economist? Well, here's your first lesson in applied business.

"Deal," I say. I figure there's no need to ask her for a guarantee regarding the committee. Besides, she couldn't make such a guarantee even if she wanted to. But I trust her, anyway. The only problem now is what would happen if for some reason we end up not getting the approval. In the meantime, we're starting work with everything still up in the air.

## 9. BETTER CLAIM THAN WORK

We meet Randy White at his house, a broad and impressive two-story structure, with an elegant combination of glass and stone. Two things are evident as soon as you step in: first, the person who lives in this house knows a thing or two about building; second, he has the money to put that knowledge to use. He's a large man, in every sense of the word, and in every direction. His dark, wrinkled skin shimmers in the soft, hidden lighting. His thick, low voice blends severity with a slight air of irony, occasionally turning into outright sarcasm. Even his name, White, seems like a pun alluding to his distinct African-American heritage.

"Gentlemen of Rhombus! Please, do come in," he welcomes us with an ironic cheer.

Randy White is what we call in professional jargon a "claimer," an expert in construction claims. Even though he is widely considered to be the best claimer in the country, this is the first time I meet him. He leads Ethan and me out to the ash-wood deck in his backyard, where a pitcher of lemonade and a couple of tall glasses are waiting for us next to a silver laptop on the table.

After sipping some lemonade and going through mandatory chitchat about the state of the market and local politics, Randy gets down to business.

"Gentlemen, when was the last time you read this contract? And I mean—all of it?"

I'm not sure what he means. Our contract with the DOT

comprises over a hundred pages. Add to that the technical breakdown, the engineering reports and the drawings, which are considered part of the contract, and all in all you're looking at about twenty boxes of material. Not exactly bedtime reading.

"You know, Randy, we have work to do," I get defensive. "Someone has to operate the site."

Ethan raises his hand slightly to intervene, but Randy gestures to say it's fine.

"My friends," he turns his laptop to us, the contract showing on its screen, "if you haven't realized it yet, it's time to understand—the contract *is* the site."

"Okay, okay, don't leave us in suspense," Ethan is anxious, "what did you find?"

With a click of a button, the patio wall slides down into the floor, revealing a huge screen mounted in the nook behind it, connected to Randy's laptop and screening an enlarged version of our contract. I steal a glance over at Ethan, who is clearly as impressed as I am by the gizmo.

"If I understand the situation correctly," he politely qualifies his statement, "you're exposed to getting sued by the client for the delay, and perhaps also by the wall contractor for terminating his project." We nod in agreement, waiting for him to reveal his hand.

"Your counterargument is that this mess with the high-voltage cable is a design issue, right?"

We both gesture for him to go on. He scrolls down the screen to page 38 and places the cursor by one of the clauses. "You see this? The contract clearly states that the client is in charge of the project's design. He authorized the drawings, he contracted TWT Planning, and so, as far as we're concerned, it's his responsibility to provide solutions to any design issue."

"We agree, of course," I say, "but is that unequivocal? I mean, I held meetings not only with TWT Planning, but with their subcontractors as well, and all of them did their best to elegantly roll the ball back to us and claim this was a construction scheduling issue, which is our responsibility."

"That's fine," Randy reassures me, "you don't expect them to say, 'I'm to blame,' right? As far as we're concerned, it makes no difference if it's the wall designer, or the road designer, or anybody with a design software who scribbled some lines on the drawings. It all comes down to the client. We deal with the DOT, and the DOT alone. Everything we have to say—or, more precisely, to write—we will address to them alone."

"They would love to take their designers' word and pin everything on us," Ethan jumps in. "Do you have something on them, as well?"

Randy answers dispassionately, "Hold on, I'm just getting started. We mentioned design, right?" he continues with the rhetorical questions, switching over to another file opened on a separate tab on his computer. He points to it and says, "This is the basic schedule you submitted for the client's approval. As you may remember, they made some minor comments which you then corrected, after which they approved it."

"And this is your contract." He switches back to the previous document. "It states that 'once the basic schedule is approved, it is appended to the contract, becoming part and parcel of the agreement...'" he pauses for a second after finishing the quote, and then says, "The schedule has very little meaning in the actual execution of the project, but that sentence makes it an extremely powerful weapon in the claims business. That's why I always handle schedules and claims together."

As an engineer, I find looking at the schedule through a pure claiming lens to be offensive. I can't help but snidely remark, "Strange. I was always under the impression that we made schedules to plan our work efficiently."

Randy retorted with sarcasm, as well, "That really is strange. Tell me, when was the last time you executed a project according to its schedule?" That response reminds me of my conversation with Nick Waters, the wall contractor. How did he put it? *None of us subcontractors take your schedule too seriously, because we know you general contractors aren't going to pay for the stops and starts you cram into it.*

I mutter something under my breath, and Randy goes on, "Unlike what they teach in college, and for several reasons we won't get into that right now, it's impossible to handle construction projects according to schedules predicated on the critical path method. It's a long explanation, so let's just skip it, but suffice it to say that the problem is not the quality of the schedule. Even when it's excellent, it still impractical."

"But that's precisely why Goldratt invented the critical chain method," I protest.

White looks at me, and for a moment I think he appreciates the fact I know what critical chain is, but he goes on to say, "Critical chain was a brilliant idea which proved very successful around the world, but not so much in the field of construction. On the contrary, when you apply the method to construction, you end up doing more harm than good…" He pauses for a moment, and says, "But let's forget about critical chain for now and focus back on your project."

"Wait, wait, wait," I jump in, slightly upset, "you're telling me that everything I know about project management is wrong, but you won't explain why?"

He sits in silence for a couple of seconds, and then says, "We're short on time, so I'll explain in a nutshell.

"Schedules are planned in advance according to assignments, not the crews that execute them," he opens. "That makes it so every crew has a string of assignments with 'gaps' between them. If the crew is already on-site, when a long 'gap' comes along, the crew needs to leave to work on a different project, and then come back. If it left to work on a different project, it won't be back until it finishes it, meaning there's no way it'll be back exactly in time to start its next assignment, meaning there's no way it keeps your schedule. The other option is that it finds something else to do on your site, for example, starting work on a task scheduled for a later date, in which case it creates a new 'gap' in the place of the mission executed ahead of time. And that's just the start of it." He looks directly into my eyes and carries on with his monologue, "Besides that, you update your schedule once a month, meaning that for twenty-nine days, your schedule is essentially overrun. Not only that, you could just as easily use it to rewrite the history of what happened during that month, and put things down that never happened in reality, because who can remember what happened a month ago?

"To finish painting the picture," he glances at me to make

sure I follow, "a couple of years back, the DOT's legal department realized that most of the claims and lawsuits it faced were rooted in schedule changes, so it started putting provisions into its contracts that in order to update the schedule during the project's lifetime, the contractor needs to obtain the owner's approval. Now, you know the DOT. To get anything approved, they need the engineering department's recommendation, budget counsel, legal counsel, and the decision of a special committee. That's a minimum of two months. So by the time those two months pass, ten new changes have already happened in practice, and there's no way to implement them into the schedule. That way, the schedule quickly loses touch with reality.

"I think that's about it. The reason I say 'about' is actually the most important part. In projects that have multiple parties involved, each party has its own interests which are incompatible with the project's interests, and each party acts according to its own interests—not the project's. These conflicts of interest influence every aspect of the project, including, among others, the schedule. Critical path and critical chain ignore these conflicts of interest. Thus, for all the reasons I just mentioned, using critical path or critical chain to plan a schedule, necessarily yields poor results when it comes to executing a project. On the other hand, when it comes to the contractor claiming against the client for causing project delays, schedules prepared using critical path or critical chain are a great tool," he concludes this didactic lecture with a sharp change of tone, saying "…which is why we're gathered here today."

To say I was left stunned would be an understatement, but

Randy White doesn't wait for me to gather my thoughts. He's quickly back on his previous train of thought, explaining what to him must seem obvious, "Your schedule contains your proposed order of operations. You can see it says nothing about relocating the cable again. Meaning, this order of operations considers the cable already relocated *before* you came onto the site. This order was approved by the client."

Ethan and I nod in approval, and he continues without pause, "Who carried out the cable's relocation? Not you. And if it wasn't you and it wasn't your responsibility, then it's the client's responsibility. If the client carried out the relocation before you constructed the wall, then he determined the order of operations. And if he determined the order of operations, he's the one to be held accountable for it. If he's accountable for the order of operations and he's also accountable for the designers, then no matter who dropped the ball—you're in the clear. That's that. That's all you needed to prove." He concluded with the air of a lecturer who just finished solving a complex mathematical equation on a whiteboard.

I'm left a bit dizzy from this compelling sequence of *if-then*'s, but I can't find any flaw in his logic. I feel a slight relief from the stress that's been weighing on me for the past few days. Ethan throws me a quick glance to say, *what did I tell you? This guy is the best*! —clear enough for me to notice, but quick enough so Randy won't use it to spike up the bill he's certain to hand us at the end of the meeting.

"How strong is this?" Ethan asks. "Is it watertight?"

"I'd love to say yes," Randy replies, "but in reality, you know how you go into a courtroom, but you never know how you're gonna come out. There's always the chance you happen to face a judge that got in a fight with his wife the night before, or something. But the bottom line is, you've got a strong case."

Despite his natural self-restraint, I can see Ethan is relieved. "What else do we need to do, and how much is this thing worth?" he asks.

Randy shrugs, and says, "There's still a lot of prep work to be done. But once I gather your logbooks, the protocols of your meetings, your correspondence with the DOT, the drawings and all their variations, etc. – I think we'll have a full crate of folders…" He pauses for emphasis, sneaks a wry smile, and says, "Those are worth about a million dollars per pound."

We chuckle in appreciation of his metaphor, but Ethan is incisive, "Do you have a figure?"

"Not yet, but I assume that after bulking it up, we can reach somewhere in the vicinity of fifteen to twenty million dollars. That's approximately what we can demand in our claim against the DOT. Now, that's only the starting price, of course. That's only where we start negotiating. Usually, these claims are settled out of court, reaching a compromise that amounts to, on average, about twenty percent of the initial sum. That's why it's important to start high." Randy smiles, and Ethan seems pleased as well. I understand why—he's finally got some kind of insurance policy over this project, which until this morning threatened to run his life's work into the ground.

***

"So, it's just a lawyers' game from this point forward?" I ask when we get back into the car.

"I hope not. Our claim is primarily a deterrence weapon. What Randy just gave us is ammunition to face the DOT, to show them that if they want to play this game in court, we've got the best team in the league. Don't worry, we're not running off to see an arbitrator or a judge tomorrow morning and, believe me, I'm not blinded by the figures he threw out there. I know we'll get a lot less than what we ask for. In the meantime, we have a road to finish, and you're in charge to see it through."

"Are you sure I can still be called project manager on this project?" I say, not hiding my bitterness. "It seems like more important decisions are made at Randy's house than in my caravan at the site."

"I'm sure, Eric. But it's good to go back to work knowing that even the worst case can turn in your favor."

## 10. SALLY ERIKSON

As I close the door after me, I feel like a teenager sneaking out of his parents' house, only this time with my kids playing the role of parents. The boys are busy with their PlayStation and Ashley's on the phone with Jayden, so I doubt anyone's going to notice I'm gone. Worst-case scenario, they'll probably think I just forgot something at the office.

I wait around my bedroom for ten minutes before Ashley finally leaves the living room and sneak out undetected. I know full well that one glance at my blue jacket and new shoes would pique her interest, resulting in a full-scale interrogation and a confession on my part, "Yes, I have a date. And yes, you've met her before."

She was on my mind for a full three days after our meeting, but I didn't have the guts to act on it. The last time I asked someone out was, well, before the kids were born. Ever since the divorce, I've gone out of my way to avoid any introductions or blind dates. Why was Sally's case different? Not on account of me.

"Hi Eric, it's Sally," she announced as I answered the phone in my office the day before yesterday. I barely managed to utter a word before she made it clear, "I'm not calling about the wall."

It was nice to hear her voice, but it was never my intention for her to ask me out. I mean, I wanted to see her, but the thought that it would be she who asked me out never even crossed my mind. This was the absolute first time I had been asked out on a date. I guess a lot has changed over the past twenty years...

When I got home that day, I regretted having immediately said yes. It's not that I wanted to play hard to get, or that I have any reservations about Sally, it's just that when I saw Ben and Josh sitting together doing their homework with a microwave dinner waiting for them on the table, I suddenly worried that maybe I didn't think it through. It's been long enough, and even Ashley has started hinting that I should move on—and yet, I felt that while they're with me, they deserve a full-time dad. Honestly, in my case it's part-time dad at best, as work already takes up so much of my time. So how do I fit a relationship into the precious little time I have left, anyway? Since I had no one to talk to about this, I played the opposite part myself. *It's just one date, you can't trigger a whole system of considerations and guilt just because a pretty woman asked you out to dinner.* I was quite convincing...

We scheduled to meet at the Blue Swan, one of those new fusion places whose menus and design are as flashy as their names, bare concrete and cold aluminum on the one hand, warm lighting and colorful dishes on the other, tall bar chairs and processed wood tables—and yet, for all its eclecticism, it blends together nicely.

Dr. Sally Erikson, my date for the evening, stands up when I approach our table, allowing me to look at her under the dim lighting, in flats and a green velvet dress, her eyes slightly accentuated with eyeliner. She's absolutely stunning.

"You beat me to it again," I smile and gesture for her to sit down.

"I hope you don't make a habit of it," she quickly retorts,

"I'm not used to being in this position."

"Neither am I," I answer instinctively. "In fact, I haven't been used to being in any position over the past few years."

"Well, I'll just update you that I've already ordered the wine. I hope Syrah is okay. That's it, you can take the lead from now on."

We chat freely, like old friends. By the second glass of wine, I am genuinely surprised by how openly I speak with a woman whom I had just met for the first time less than a week ago. I tell her about Karen and our divorce, about the kids and how difficult it was to be the father they deserve, and even about my non-dates and my apprehension ahead of this date. She has something insightful to say after everything I say, and when she says nothing, she just smiles gently – the soft gaze of her mesmerizing eyes says all that needs to be said.

I am relieved to learn she has her own doubts, as well. "You know, I've never been on a date with a contractor before," she casually remarks. I don't know if I'm supposed to take offense to that, so I just chuckle. "Neither have I."

"No, really. Every meeting I have with contractors I always get the feeling they think I'm trying to dupe them, and they never believe a single word I say. It's really exhausting. That wasn't the case with you."

"That's only because you managed to dupe me in the end."

"Why? Didn't you get the wall you came for?"

"I did. And I even got a date with a beautiful woman. I guess I did do something right, after all. I just hope you won't extort me again this time."

"Don't worry, no more tricks. Good?"

Even though we agreed not to talk business during the date, after the food arrives, I start to tell her about the 612 and our other projects. She surprises me with her extensive knowledge of the field. She obviously knows the design aspects well, but even when we discuss materials and management strategies, she doesn't miss a step. In contrast, when it's her turn to tell me about projects she managed or advised, I need several pauses to clarify some terms that are new to me.

Without noticing, over three hours pass. It's only when the waiter informs us that they're about to close the kitchen that we realize we're practically the last people in an otherwise empty restaurant.

I have no idea who sat at the tables next to us, what the bartender looked like, or even what we ordered for starters. I was fully focused on Sally the entire evening. I was as absorbed in her as I am absorbed in my work when I'm working, forgetting the outside world exists. I insist to pick up the check, despite her protest. "You said I could take the lead, didn't you?"

I take my time paying, trying to prolong the evening as much as I can. I'm a bit lost as to what to do next.

"Would you like to walk me to my car?" she sees through me. I quickly help her put her short black jacket on.

A hybrid car—what did I expect?—is parked next to my gas-guzzling Land Cruiser. "We'll talk about this camel you call a car next time," she remarks, pointing at a bumper sticker bearing Rhombus' logo which quickly gives me away.

"So, there's going to be a next time?"

"If you ask me."

## 11. THE DESIGNER'S INTERESTS

After the party wraps up, and his best friends, Adam and Brady, leave, Josh comes up to me with a big smile on his face, "This was the best birthday I've had since... since the divorce." I hug him tightly and thank the lord that my children manage to find happiness in their lives. It's been three years since Karen and I split up, and today, when he is twelve years old, I realize that he has spent a large part of life living between two houses, trying to remain loyal to both his mother and father while somehow keeping his head above water.

"Can I go up to my room to open my presents?"

"Of course, buddy. Take Ben with you. Me and Aunt Danielle will tidy up a bit."

A bit? 33 sixth-graders just ran amok in my living room and balcony. My house looks like it's been hit by a tsunami. Doritos and potato-chip crumbs are everywhere, and sticky soda stains cover every surface, while torn and discarded gift and snack wrappers litter the floor.

"That went well, didn't it?" I feel Danielle's arm over my shoulder. As I turn around to answer yes, she hugs me. I have no idea how I'd have managed without her today. It's not just the shopping and the food, or the presents she brought, but mainly those instances she was there to intervene right before an argument between two kids erupted into a fight that would have spoiled the party. Looking at her from a distance, I feel a bit sad she doesn't have children of her own.

I want to tell her what a great mother she would be, but I decide not to say anything. On this subject, we always keep our thoughts to ourselves.

"It went excellent, Danielle. I couldn't have done it without you."

This whole day has been a bit too much for me. Thoughts of yesterday's great date with Sally intermixed with nagging concerns about work, and the preparations for Josh's party in the evening. To top it all off, I received a phone call this morning from Martin Chambers of the DOT.

"Congratulations, Price," he opened without any introductions, "remember the tender for role of chief engineer?" To be honest, at the moment, I had no idea what he was talking about. I was going over the shopping list for Josh's party again; he had made me swear I wouldn't forget anything, or his party would be ruined. "What? Who is this?" I asked absentmindedly. By the time I realized it was Chambers, he had informed me I won the bid.

With everything I had going on at that moment, I simply couldn't take anything else on board, let alone something as huge as that.

"L-Listen, Mr. Chambers," I stuttered a bit, "I can't really talk right now. Could we talk at the start of next week?"

"Price, do you hear what I'm saying?" he sounded surprised, and perhaps a bit offended. "I'm offering you the opportunity of a lifetime. To be chief engineer. To be the one who calls the shots with an annual budget of two billion dollars. To influence every single project that goes on here. This is what you wanted when you interviewed for the job, isn't it? To be able to influence, think into the future and plan for the long-term, all without the pressures of the private sector or the constant tit for tat with subcontractors and suppliers. And let's not forget public sector benefits and conditions, and the freedom to leave your work at the office over the weekend without having to give them so much as another thought."

He didn't have to remind me why I wanted this job so badly a couple of months back.

"That really is great news, but I need a minute to process this, okay? I mean, the DOT doesn't rush decisions anyway, right?"

"Usually, yes, but this time it's different," I'm surprised to hear him say. "It turns out Biden's wife has severe health issues. Long story short, he informed us he's terminating his work immediately, catching us completely off guard. In practice, we have been without a chief engineer for the past twenty-four hours. We need this position manned as quickly as possible. Because of the urgency of the matter, the governor authorized me to bring in whomever I choose…" He lingers for a second and says, "And I want you. You're the only candidate who has real work experience in the contracting world. All the other candidates were reared in the public sector. They're good guys, but they don't understand the mindset of the private sector, so they won't be able to implement the changes we want to see."

I was flattered, but the idea of leaving Ethan without notice after all the years we'd been working together is not something I could contemplate at the moment. "I see. By when do you need an answer?"

"Tomorrow morning. And even that is just because I am

a very patient person."

"Let's talk at the start of next week, I promise to give you my final answer."

It's a strange situation, the person I would usually turn to when weighing such a decision is Ethan, but when the consequence of me taking this job is leaving him without notice, even he wouldn't be able to give me unbiased advice.

The state of the living room fittingly reflects my state of mind; I look around at the mess, and I don't even know where to start. I wish I could just leave everything as it is until tomorrow, but Martha, the maid, won't be here until Friday, and I can't just ignore this mess. Danielle reads my mind. "Okay, this is what we'll do—you pick up the pizza boxes and empty bottles and throw them away outside. Meanwhile, I'll start cleaning the tables. Okay?"

I finish rounding up filthy pizza boxes and empty plastic bottles from the floor, trails of molten cheese, crumbs and a sticky floor remain. When I get back, Danielle is ready with my next assignment, "Now, take a large garbage bag and fill it with all the disposable plates and cups lying around here."

"Yes, sir," I try to tease her, but she's not bothered.

"Start with the balcony. I want to wash the floor there."

After I finish filling two bags with plates doused in tomato sauce and food coloring, and plastic cups filled with flat soda, I take the bags outside to the trash cans. I do damage-control and scour the lawn for discarded trash, then return to put dishes in the dishwasher, and clean the counter. When I'm finally done, I turn and see Danielle looking at me as she sets down the mop and bucket. "I think we pretty much have this under control," she smiles.

When Ashley heads out, I invite Danielle for a grown-up conversation. She readily agrees, adding that such an event calls for props. She goes over to the kitchen cupboard and returns with two glasses—red wine for her, Johnny Walker on the rocks for me. She sits down beside me. "What's going on, Eric? This project is really draining you, isn't it?"

"It's not just that," I reply. "Remember a couple of months back that I applied for the position of chief engineer at the DOT?"

"Sure. We even talked about it, and I suggested you give it a try. But what does that have to do with anything?"

"Chambers called me this morning. Long story short, I have two days to give him an answer."

"Wow, Eric, that's big news!" she looks at me, trying to gauge whether this is a cause for celebration, or if it only makes matters worse.

"It is big news. The problem is, I have no idea what to decide."

"What about Ethan," she hits the nail right on the head, "did you speak with him?"

"What would I say? 'Help me decide whether I should abandon you without notice in the middle of the biggest project of the company's history'? I can't do that," I finish my whiskey in one gulp, and get up to pour another glass.

"Besides Ethan, what other reasons do you have not to take it? You must have made those calculations already when you first applied for the job. You wanted to have influence where it really matters, take a bit of the pressure off yourself, and be able to come home to the kids at a reasonable hour. Has anything changed?"

"Nothing's changed for me, but I just came in to save the 612. Abandoning the project now feels like betrayal. Not to mention Ethan."

"Eric, I know that road almost as well as you do. Over the past six months, it's been through countless changes and disruptions, and yet the company is still alive. I don't mean to offend your ego, but the road, and Ethan as well, will survive without you. You're not going to bring down the company, if that's what you're worried about."

That's the best thing about consulting someone who knows you from childhood. They won't let you believe your own exaggerations. "I think you're right," I hesitantly say, but before I go on, she perceptively sees I have yet to cross the Rubicon and adds, "And don't worry about Ethan. He'll be fine. He was fine before you came along, and he'll be fine after you're gone. Not only that, I think that if you tell him you're going to be the DOT's chief engineer, he'll recognize the advantage of having a friend at the top. At least, that's what I would think if I were him."

Touché, Danielle. She's a quick thinker, my sister. I don't have anything to say in response, but I'm still uncertain. "I think I need to sleep on it," I finally reply.

"Take your time," she answers quickly. "You have two nights, don't you?"

After a couple of seconds of silence, I change the subject and tell her about the meeting with Randy White, how we read the contract together, the solutions he proposed, and how not a single one of them had anything to do with streamlining the project, but rather about its legal aspects.

"Well, the things this claimer says are sensible. Even in my field, that's how things actually work."

"Meaning?"

"Meaning that until the moment the contract is signed, we will do anything for our client. We will happily commit to painting the moon in zebra stripes, if that's what would make him sign the order. Once the contract is signed, it's a completely different tune. Since we took the contact for practically no profit, we now do everything in our power to not to do what we committed to doing without breaching our contract and dealing with the legal ramifications."

"What do you mean?" I ask. "I know contractors always have problems with the client, but I thought that wasn't the case with designers. I mean, you're on the client's side." Her smile conveys something between irony and pity. "Are you really that oblivious, Eric? How could we possibly be on the client's side? We have a contract with him." Since I still don't get it, I throw out a feeler, "What exactly do you mean? Give me an example."

"Come on, Eric. Literally anything could be an example, from the initial drawings to the final version."

"Still," I implore her.

"Take the first drawing, the earliest design we put out. Because it is very preliminary, intended only to decide which direction we're going to pursue, we are supposed to present three options, so that the client could compare and choose the best option."

"That makes sense," I say.

"Right. But logic would also tell you that the client makes his choices based on economic considerations, and for him to get a general appreciation of the three options, we need to develop them to a pretty advanced level. A level that will allow the client to ascertain their cost." She sees I am nodding and goes on, "And logic would also tell you that planning three options costs three time more than planning one option—"

"You mean to tell me you don't submit three options?"

"Of course we do. After all, we have a contract that says that in order for us to be paid for the preliminary planning, we need to present three options. So we submit three. But we only detail one of those options—the one we consider in advance to be the best. The other two, we pretend. We churn out a couple of drawings that show why they are less desirable or too expensive, and that's it."

"That sounds risky. Doesn't the client ever catch on to the fact you're not actually doing your job?" I try to push her, but she surprises me again.

"The best part is when someone does. Usually, that some- one is the contractor, who looks at the drawings with com- pletely different eyes than the client. When he finds an al- ternative, something that we missed but could reduce costs, he files a request with the client to alter the original drawing with a drawing of his own that would save the project time or money. The client is of course pleased, since the money saved is split between him and the contractor, but in order to be certain the alternative is legitimate, he runs it to his con- sultant—that being us…" She pauses to inhale, and delivers the punchline, "That way, we get paid in the beginning to do a job we perform only partially, and get paid a second time to double-check the contractor whose proposed changes should have been proposed by us in the first place. Pretty similar to what's happening now with your 612."

# PART 2 | THE GOAL FUNCTION

## 12. CHAMBERS' VISION

My first day starts off with a serious talk with Chambers. It's our first serious conversation since that surprising phone call two weeks ago, which ended up with me working for the DOT.

My work agreement with Ethan stated I had to notify three months in advance before resigning. But it didn't take Chambers more than twenty minutes to convince him to forgo that. Even though Chambers didn't commit to anything, Ethan took his word that he would help him come out of the whole 612 mess unscathed if he allowed me to go immediately. And here I am.

After (concise) congratulations and a (brief) courtesy question—"how are the kids?"—he gets down to business. "Do you see these?" he points to a stack of about fifty medium-sized booklets lying on the shelf behind him. "Don't bother going over them now, you'll have plenty of time over the coming days."

I glance at their titles, "BJ Engineering vs. DOT et al.,;" "Green Inc. vs. DOT," and others in the same vain. Printed and bound statements of claims by contractors against the DOT, meaning against us, the owner who commissioned the work. "These are just from the past year, and there are more," he looks at me to gauge if I catch his drift.

"I'm the manager of a body that's supposed to build things.

To expand the country's infrastructure in order to improve people's quality of life. I know how to do that, and, if I say so myself, I'm not half bad at it. But over the past two decades, this place has started to resemble a law firm more than a construction business. We get claims for making changes in over ninety percent of our projects. A third of those make it to arbitration or court. I can safely estimate that no less than a quarter of this office's work hours is dedicated entirely to dealing with or preventing these claims, and a quarter more is dedicated to producing a paper trail to prove we acted by the book." He takes a break to emphasize he's reached the bottom line, "And all this effort contributes absolute zilch toward our actual product, which, at the end of the day, is concrete and asphalt."

I keep scouring the pile of booklets and notice a couple of familiar names—contractors, projects our company didn't win, and even Randy White, the claimer, is there.

"Well," I say, "you probably have a whole legal team here to handle contractor claims. I guess that doesn't really concern me."

Wasting no time, he gives what seems to be an answer he's prepared in advance, "Price, it's clear from your résumé that you are a great engineer, but that's not why I made such an effort to bring you here. I don't need you because you know how to build roads, but because you understand the mindset of those who build them. You're here because you know the other side. You know how a contractor thinks because you've spent a lot of time among them. I have enough engineers here, some of whom are very good. I also have a battery of lawyers who know what they're doing. My problem is that

neither my engineers nor my lawyers seem to be able to prevent us from getting constantly dragged to court. If we're
lucky, after three years of court hearings, I get invited for
a toast to celebrate a judge having ruled in our favor. And
just to be clear, when they say we won and that a judge has
ruled in our favor, they mean that out of a million dollars
the contractor asked for, the judge ruled he should only get
a quarter of million—a quarter of a million that we pay, of
course. You see, even our victories are nothing more than
curtailed losses. I want this pile halved by next year, and
in three years' time, I want the dealing with claims to be
minimal. You see what I'm saying?"

"Um, I think so," I reply, even though I don't really catch
his drift. I'm an engineer, what do I know about arbitration
and courtrooms? "Basically, you want these cases resolved
faster?"

"No," he smiles, as if he anticipated my question, "I want
you to use your understanding of the other side to find a way
to prevent these claims from being served in the first place.
To find a way to get us back to where we were thirty-five
years ago, when I started working in this office. I want to go
back to being the one who builds bridges and paves roads in
the most efficient way possible, not the one who wins claims
because he successfully proved the inefficiency was someone
else's fault."

"How do you even start going about that?" I ask, realizing
that my job might actually turn to be quite different than
what I thought when I walked into this office a couple of
minutes ago.

"The first thing to understand is that this office doesn't

manage projects, it manages contracts. Contracts to design projects, contracts to execute projects, contracts to manage projects, contracts for measurements, contracts to check the ground, etc., etc. What we do is draw up and manage contracts that define what those who design and execute these projects themselves are supposed to be doing. We put into these contracts what we want them to do and how we plan to pay them to do it. The problem is that apparently we're not very good at drawing up these contracts, because everyone we work with turns out to be double agents. The day after we sign the contract, they all start asking themselves how they can squeeze more money out of us for the same work we already negotiated for and agreed on its price the day before. To defend ourselves, our lawyers draw up increasingly one-sided, draconian agreements, so much so that I sometimes ask myself if the contracts are legal—but even that doesn't help. We keep receiving claims, time and time again."

"You mean to tell me that no matter how draconian a contract may be, it doesn't change the number of claims filed?" I ask in surprise.

"Even worse. Since our new contracts try to pin all the risk on the contractor, the result is that we often get claims that we could perhaps legally fight and win, but that we all feel would ethically be wrong and unfair toward him. At that stage, our legal advisers recommend that I 'buy the risk' the contractor would win in court. That's their legal way to pay him for not filing a claim against our unreasonable contract, rather than paying him to do his job. Drawing up a hard contract and then 'buying the risk' of a claim makes about as much sense as counting calories during dinner and then splurging on dessert. At the end of the day, we end up paying more."

"How do you know we end up paying more?"

"It's simple, really," he answers, "the profit margin in the contracting business is about four percent of the cycle, and what determines this margin is not the hardness of the contract but the ancient rule of supply and demand. In every tender, contractors offer prices that allow them to compete with other contractors. On average, those prices cover their costs and leave them some profit. When we add legal expenses to the contractor's engineering expenses, he simply adds that to his bid."

"I don't think that's right," I say. "I've prepared dozens of bids, and I've never included projected legal expenses to the offer. At that stage, you're trying to draw up as low an offer as you possibly can to give you the best chance of winning the tender, so you base your calculations on optimistic projections, like, for example, not having legal expenses."

"I'm afraid that changes very little," he says. "Your company might have labeled legal expenses under 'overhead' because they are designated as company expenditure, rather than the project's expenditure. You might not have included those expenses in your proposal because you assumed there would be profits not included in the offer as well, that would offset those expenses. But either way, it's the same result. Our contracts create legal expenses which increase the cost of the project. I'm afraid the problem might actually be even bigger than that. When instead of paying a contractor for his work we pay for 'buying risk' or a settlement agreement, we distort the market. In practice, we prioritize contractors who are specialists in filing claims and squeezing the most out of us in settlements, at the expense of contractors who only know how to work and issue invoices for the engineering services they performed—even though we'd like it be the other way around."

"You know," I say, "Ethan McKey used to always tell me that owners force contractors to become crooks, and then complain about our dishonesty."

"And that's not all," Chambers goes on, "because we pin the responsibility on the contractor, we let the project manager and designers off the hook. Subsequently, we turn the contractors into crooks and make the project managers careless and complacent. When I look around me, I see stagnation. We haven't improved the quality of our design in twenty years, even though a whole bunch of new technologies have emerged that were supposed to do just that. And forget about the quality of project management. I hope I'm not just being a nostalgic old fool, but when I got into this business, before we had online communication for every project and two legal consultants for each engineer, the quality of management and decision-making was better. Everyone knew exactly who was in charge, and it was clear that person had to be decisive in his decision-making, because there were crews and equipment in the field waiting for his decisions. Today, every single decision takes longer, and its quality is calibrated by the extent of the legal cover it provides for someone else's ass, rather than its contribution to the project."

The conversation must be taking longer than planned, because Chambers glances at his watch and tries to conclude.

"We're nothing special. These same troubles are found everywhere, not only in our country, and I am assuming the main issue is that we don't understand the problem to its fullest extent. That's why I brought you in. You know how the other side thinks, so I'm hoping you can bring new ideas to the table."

His monologue leaves me feeling a bit embarrassed. "I thank you for the credit," I say, "and I really hope it will prove to be prudent in hindsight. But to be completely honest, I don't have the faintest idea how to even start going about this. You see, I've filed claims against an owner many times, even when I honestly felt we didn't deserve that payment, but I always did it because those were the rules of the game. I've never given thought to how those rules could be changed."

"I've scheduled a lunch for you with two important people around here, that would be a good starting point on this journey. They'll come to your office in a couple of hours. Until then, pop over to HR and IT, and get settled into your office. Okay?"

I do just that, until Greg knocks on my door and invites me to lunch.

## 13. THE OWNER'S TAKE ON REALITY

It's been a while since I've last sat in the backseat of a car. It's 1 p.m. on my first day as a government employee, and I sit in the middle of the backseat, leaning slightly forward in order to chat with my two new colleagues. The driver is Naomi—attorney Naomi Griffin—a handsome and serious woman is her late forties. Wearing a black pant suit and a large black hairpin holding her hair up in a bun, she speaks in short, dry sentences—concise, but enough for me to understand she is sharp. If she was hiding a smile during the few minutes we spent chatting, she hid it well. When introducing us, Chambers described her as the "best public service legal counsel in a thousand-mile radius"; she tilted her head and slightly raised the black frame of her glasses in response, while asking if he ever checked further than that, because he'd have a hard time finding anyone better there as well.

Sitting next to her is Greg Nader, who reclined his seat back slightly and is now humming an unfamiliar tune. From where I sit, I can just make out the tip of his slicked back silver fringe, and the expensive watch (or so it seems) he wears on his left wrist. The DOT's chief financial officer turns out to be a pleasant and talkative person, despite a deep stress wrinkle running down his forehead. "I just hope you'll stick around," he says without looking back at me, "there are not many lunches we can invest in new people joining this office."

I think I've already got the measure of this man, but I want to make sure he's joking, "Well, that depends on where you're taking me, doesn't it?"

"Appleby's," he retorts and is quick to explain, "because fast food is too lowbrow, and a bistro is too expensive." Naomi nods her head in agreement without taking her eyes off the road.

I'll have to get used to these two's nuances.

\*\*\*

We sit down, me on one side and my new colleagues next to each other on the opposite side of the table.

"You have to try the Caesar salad," Greg says enthusiastically, and turns to Naomi, "isn't it great?"

"Greg tends to exaggerate, not only when it comes to work matters. But yes, the Caesar salad's not bad."

"Come on Naomi, is there any dish more fitting for a new chief engineer?"

I'm unsure what kind of ritual I've found myself a part of, but I have a feeling these two are calculated in their words, so I keep quiet. Every project I've ever worked on, I've had the habit of keeping quiet and letting others speak first. I didn't always accept or agree with what was being said, but I knew introductory periods were always tests. I preferred being the examiner than the examinee.

The food arrived. We discussed the area, and the new schools in the county. Greg took an interest in my previous job, "So, you could say you were a contractor?"

"Not exactly. I was chief engineer of a contracting company, but never wanted to take the leap to open my own company."

"You were absolutely right. Who needs that headache? Whenever I meet contractors in budget meetings, they always look like they're on the brink of collapse. They try to maintain a veneer of confidence, but it doesn't take more than one or two clauses to be concluded against them for the cracks to starts showing."

"I completely agree with Greg," Naomi interjects after sipping her iced tea, "sometimes I feel like the essence of being a contractor is having your mood dial, the one in charge balancing between *fight or flight* modes, permanently stuck on *fight*. I don't think they enjoy it, but it's like they don't know any other way to conduct themselves."

"Good thing I'm not a real contractor, then," I try to joke, squeezing two meager smiles from my dining partners.

"To be honest, you don't act like a contractor, either," Greg adds.

"And what does acting like a contractor mean, exactly?" I can't hold back any longer. I have to remind myself that I don't want to sour this relationship right from the start.

"Oh, you know," Greg struggles to find the words. "It's just different with you."

This guy might be great with numbers, but when it comes to composing sentences, he's not the sharpest tool in the shed. "I think I know what he's trying to say," Naomi jumps in to help him. "It always feels like contractors conduct themselves with a slight dishonesty. You always get the feeling that no matter what the contract says, they'll find some way to wriggle out of sticking to their word, and somehow flip it to make it seem like it's all your fault."

I think I'm starting to see why Chambers set up this lunch.

"I'm sorry to spoil your idea of contractors, but the contractor I worked for over the past twenty years never acted like that. In fact, he's one of the most honest and attentive people I've ever met in my life," I'm quick to defend Ethan and the professional world I came from. But as I'm speaking, I can't help but recall the reinforced soil wall and the conversation with Nick Waters, the wall contractor. That's exactly what he said—contracts are signed knowing in advance they are going to be broken.

"I didn't mean anything personal by it," Naomi switches her gaze from Greg to me. "I'm just drawing on personal experience. I know Chambers spoke with you about trying to prevent claims, and that's great. But for now, I'm just focused on trying to win the ones we're already involved in."

"Of course, that's your job," I try to wrap up this topic, "and from what I've heard, you're not half bad at it." Greg casually nods along to my blatant attempt at flattery.

"You know Eric, it's not my job to deal with these threats and claims," he says, "but the way contractors conduct their business is driving me and everyone at the office mad. Do you know what it's like to try to stick to a budget when the financial landscape keeps shifting because of incessant arbitrations and claims?"

"Actually, I don't," I admit, "but it doesn't sound like fun."

"At the end of the day, we are bound by budget constraints. We're allocated a certain sum in advance, and we have to make do with that. Every time I go to the governor's office in the middle of a project to ask for additional funds to pay for some unexpected change, they look at me like some sort of clueless idiot who doesn't know how to run a project. You try explaining that when engineers plan a two-year project, they can't foresee all the problems along the way. Later, when those problems turn up, they are solved—but always at a cost."

"Of course," I say. "Uncertainty is always part of the game. There's nothing to do about that."

To my surprise, his hitherto soft tone suddenly turns sterner. He seems to be venting things that have been on his mind for some time.

"I don't believe that. When you say uncertainty is part of the game, what you're doing in fact is giving everybody a license to cut corners. Designers, consultants, contractors—the lot. What you're saying is that we have to assume responsibility over their uncertainties, and I don't see any reason why that should be. Why shouldn't they be one hundred percent responsible for their own work? Not eighty, not ninety. One hundred percent. If they knew those were the rules of the game, first, they would do a better job, and second, their initial tender would already incorporate those risks."

He pauses for a moment and takes a sip of water, as if to cool himself down, and reverts back to the calculated tone of an accountant. "For me to be able to run a budget well, I need the contractors to be responsible for changes. I need their initial tender to include all the variables, I can't have them adding expenses a second after the contract has been signed because this nuance or that wasn't included in their projections."

I decide to play devil's advocate. "But what if our designs change during the process? That's what contractors usually say—that what we ask for now is not what we asked for in the beginning." As I speak, I marvel at how quickly and naturally the word *us* has changed it meaning for me. First it was *us, the contractor* duking it out with the thick-headed bureaucracy of the client. Now, a mere couple of hours later, it's already *us—the owner* valiantly defending ourselves against unscrupulous contractors trying to take us for a ride. This time, he takes a moment before giving his answer.

"What I want is to buy the entire project from the contractors, including insurance against any unexpected changes that might come up along the way. Of all the different parties involved in the project, it's the contractors who have the most knowledge and experience of what can go wrong and why. I'm not looking for any free rides—I'm more than willing to pay for this insurance. But I want them to include these potential recalibrations and changes in their initial tender. What I don't want is to be handed a bill in the end."

As someone who has spent his entire career on the side of the contractor, I had to contend with the owner's finance people on many occasions. But I had never stopped to reflect that, in fact, they are also contending with an opponent, and that their concerns are very similar to mine—they are concerned with proving they're not responsible for unforeseen changes.

"Did you ever try drawing up a contract that requires the contractor to give us that insurance?" I ask.

"I tried," his mouth contracts into a small, tired smile, "I asked our insurance consultant to draw up something like that, but that lazy bastard says it can't be done."

"Why?"

"He says that in order to price an insurance policy, he has

to define and delineate precisely what risks it covers, the likelihood of those risks happening, and the scale of reparations due, while I want the exact opposite—a plan to cover all the risks I can't foresee, can't define, and can't delineate. Also, he says that what I'm asking is for the contractor to provide insurance, not against him not doing his job properly, but against the risk that we and the designers don't do our jobs right. He says that we are the ones that have to provide that insurance, not the contractor."

I can see Naomi smirking across the table. "I'm not an expert in risk insurance," she interjects, "but you have to understand that the primary concern we have to deal with is the contractor's claims. We have to phrase our contracts in a way that will help us win the legal battles that are sure to ensue later, when the contractors file their claims. Every single clause in the contract presupposes the end point of the process and is phrased in a way that will help us win."

"Like how?" I ask.

"That's simple," she answers immediately. "First, I avoid conceding any distinct rights and privileges to the contractor and avoid assuming direct responsibility over anything if I don't absolutely have to. Additionally, I instruct our designers and project managers to never take any direct responsibility either, and throw it back to the contractors instead. Being as vague as possible and refusing to take responsibility gives us much more managerial flexibility, later."

The terms she is using are so far from the world of engineering I've spent my entire life in, that I honestly don't understand what she means. I don't feel comfortable revealing my ignorance, so instead I ask what she means by "managerial flexibility."

She doesn't drop her veil of sarcasm for even a second and replies immediately, "Oh, that's simple. When contractors know that whether they get paid or not hinges on my good will, they are much more user-friendly."

I'm struggling to hold back what I really think and have to constantly remind myself that amicability is more important than honesty right now. I settle on a measured response and say, "I'm surprised to hear what you are saying. Not because you are suspicious of contractors but by the intensity of that suspicion. You speak about them like they're your enemies."

Naomi and Greg exchange glances and remain silent for a couple of seconds.

"Eric, you need to understand," the CFO says, the man with whom I'm destined to spend many hours working alongside, "things look different from this side. You may be used to valuating projects in terms of deadlines and quality of execution, but two days on the job and you'll start to see the bigger picture. Contractors are not the enemy, but they are certainly adversaries—because their interests are in direct opposition to ours. For them to make money, we need to lose. And for us to not lose too much, Naomi does what she does. Don't forget, at the end of the day, we are protecting public funds. A great, great deal of public funds."

Naomi picks up the check. I don't ask any questions, and politely thank her for the meal. "Don't worry about it," Greg reads my mind, "eventually, that receipt will soon be on my desk under 'business meal expense,' or something like that."

I'll have to get used to that, as well.

## 14. RED-HANDED

The morning starts like some sort of romantic comedy cliché. I walk into the kitchen after taking a shower, and Sally is already standing there, wearing only an oversized T-shirt she found in my closet and cooking breakfast. According to the rules of the genre, there should have been pancakes and coffee on the table, perhaps bacon and eggs, but instead, Dr. Erikson pours me a glass of a pale, greenish liquid, a smile stretched across her face. "Here you go. The vegan omelet will be ready in a minute."

"That's an unusual-looking cup of coffee," I remark with a smile on my face. I put my arm around her shoulder.

"Would you like me to quote some research over the benefits of green tea and how much healthier it is than coffee, or do you wanna just drink in peace?"

"Yes, ma'am," I reply and feign a shamed expression.

An unfamiliar folk song is playing in the background. Sally notices my confusion and picks up her cell phone. "I paired it to your Bluetooth speakers. I hope that's alright."

The vegan omelet resembles a regular omelet about as much as the green tea resembles coffee, but I don't care. After such a wonderful night, the kind I had forgotten was even possible, we could have shoes for breakfast for all I care.

The surprising thing about Sally is how quickly things move with her. I don't mean in the physical sense, which is great in itself; after our first date, I had prepared myself for a long process. *Take things slow; no need to rush; let things happen at their own pace*—all these things I had told myself simply became irrelevant as soon as we started seeing each other. It's like she has this superpower which speeds up time, completely changing the rhythm of life. In any other situation, I'd beat myself up for letting my guard down so fast, but she makes everything so easy and effortless.

"I see the omelet is not quite to your liking. Would you prefer some cereal, or some other commercial product instead?" I can see her struggling to hold back her scorn for processed foods.

"Sally, we said in advance that we're going to have to get used to some changes, right? So, you take the lead on this one, from now on, when we're together, no more processed foods. Okay?"

"That's less the extent of my vision, but I'll settle on it for a start. Don't worry, when I'm done with you, we'll grow our own food in the garden outside our house."

"What house?" I laugh, but I tense up a bit from the sudden turn in the conversation.

"What do you mean, why do you think I'm dating an engineer? Aren't you going to build us the house of our dreams?"

Good god, what is she talking about? We've barely known each other for three weeks. On the other hand, I can easily envision that house. Single floor, high ceilings, two small guestrooms, a large study, and a master bedroom; thin window profiles, a large garden surrounding the house, and a paved path curling behind it. "And what do I get in return? A vegan burger? Dairy-free soymilk ice cream?" I lean in for a long kiss.

"Don't worry," she pushes me back slightly, "I'll make it

worth your while." We stand there for a long time, holding each other and looking in each other's eyes. We don't say anything, but we mean everything. The music keeps playing in the background. We kiss again, oblivious to time passing, the microwave beeping, and the front door opening.

"Dad, I'm here!" I hear Ashley calling from the lobby, and freeze in my spot. She breezes into the kitchen and sees us, her face dons an expression I've never seen before.

"Ashely," I mutter, and can't add a single word. Sally stands still as well, her face flushed. It's clear to see she is embarrassed.

"I-I just wanted to pick up a sweatshirt for school," Ashley says and stares at the floor. "Mom and the boys are waiting outside."

I hear Ben shouting to his sister to hurry up because they're running late, and a second later, he appears at the door as well.

"Well, this is getting awkward," I say and try to muster a smile, but Ben doesn't say anything and just stares at Sally. "Kids, this is Sally," I say, unsure how to introduce her. Not that anyone has any doubt what's going on…

"Yes, we've met," Ashley suddenly says, and I can't make out if she's being sarcastic or if she's genuinely amused. She's probably not amused—this is not the ideal way to meet the first woman your divorced father has dated since the divorce. Ben, in contrast, is much more direct. Without saying a word, he turns and leaves, not bothering to close the door behind him.

"Well, I don't want to keep Mom waiting," Ashley wraps up this awkward encounter, "I'll see you tonight, right?"

"What?"

"This evening. We're with you. You remember, right?"

"Oh, s-sure."

I hear the door slam. I take a deep breath and close my eyes. When I open them, I see Sally standing in front of me, looking at me with a serious expression. "I need to get to work, Eric." She is fully dressed, and I don't understand at what point she managed to slip away during the awkward encounter with Ashley and Ben.

"At least we passed the stage of meeting the family," I try to joke, but Sally's not smiling anymore. She walks out, leaving behind her an air of uneasiness where a breezy and carefree atmosphere pervaded just a few minutes earlier.

I think about Ashely, Ben, and Josh, and even Karen who must been informed by now about the woman in the kitchen and my oversized shirt she was wearing.

My kids are old enough to know that this day was going to come. Karen even beat me in the all-too-well-known contest among divorcees—who's the first to bring a new partner home. And yet Ashley's look and Ben's reaction convey a different message.

## 15. JAYDEN'S DILEMMA

I open the front door and walk absentmindedly to the kitchen to get a beer from the fridge, when I stumble on a bag strewn on the floor. I look over to the living room and see that I'm not alone. Jayden and Ashley are on the couch, looking at me like I just walked in on something I wasn't supposed to see. And maybe that was indeed the case.

"Dad, what are you doing here?"

"What am I doing here? Why don't you rethink that question?"

"Right. I forgot you get back at this hour, now. My shift at Tom's got canceled, so Jayden came over."

"Hello, Mr. Price," he says. What a stark contrast between the killer on the court and the reserved, shy boy outside it.

"I hope I'm not interrupting," I say, only to hear Ashley quickly retort, "It's fine. We're even now." She's a bit impudent, but it's hard not to be impressed by her sharp thinking. I look at Jayden and hope he didn't hear about what happened here this morning. But by the way he diverts his gaze, I realize that's probably not the case.

I offer them something to drink. When Ashley asks for an apple juice and a snack as well, I seize the opportunity to say, "Come help me in the kitchen, then."

She enters the kitchen with visible unease. I assume I look pretty much the same.

"Okay, sweetie, let's get this out of the way. Okay?" She

nods in agreement and seems to be a bit taken aback by my directness.

She explains what she felt this morning, and I'm somewhat relieved to discover she wasn't as shocked by the situation as I had feared. She says she suspected I might be seeing someone but didn't want to pry. She even thought it might be Sally, because, "you two didn't stop flirting the whole time that day." Yes, the unplanned encounter this morning was embarrassing, especially when Ben walked in and later told Josh and Karen (I would actually love to have seen her face), and she spent most of the day thinking about it, but she concluded by saying, "All in all, I'm cool with it."

"So, I can skip the restaurant I had planned for the evening, then. Right?"

"What? No! What about the boys? Give them something nice to remember about this day."

I know we have a lot more to talk about, questions that need answering—like, are Sally and me a couple? What are the chances of us moving in together? What do her kids think about me? Honestly, these were things I needed to figure out for myself, first.

"So, how are you, Jayden?" I change the subject as I walk into the living room with a beer and a bag of nacho chips.

"I'm fine, sir," he looks over at Ashley, not sure what's about to happen.

"How's your ankle? I heard from Ashley you got back to training last week." I really was happy to hear that. Everyone who was in the stadium that day remembers his fall, and even though it seemed like he'd be sidelined for months, Jayden got back on his ankle in no time. He's not playing yet, a fact which makes my weekends significantly more convenient, no chauffeuring, and none of Ashley's stress to deal with.

"It's going well so far," he leans forwards slightly, "my physiotherapist must have done a good job." I like this kid's optimism. Not everyone would've handled that injury so gracefully.

"So did you, babe," Ashley adds and hugs him. "You earned it."

Jayden tells me about his first steps back on the court, his apprehension before leaping for the first time, and his relief to see his ankle was fine. "He can't play competitively yet," Ashley is quick to clarify, "the doctor says he needs at least another two weeks out, but we're super happy so far." *We*, she says. Like's it's a joint project.

"It feels fine to me, and Coach wants me already playing by Sunday. Columbus High are coming, and you know what that means, right?" He turns to Ashley.

The smile disappears from her face. She places her hand on Jayden's left thigh. "Don't rush it, okay?"

I observe the two of them and can't help but notice the sudden tension between them. There's a certain stiffness in Ashley's voice and in Jayden's facial muscles.

"So, where do you guys want to go for dinner?" I try to break the tension by changing the subject, "I'm paying this time…"

Ashley doesn't laugh, and Jayden gets up and grabs his backpack. "Thank you very much, sir, but I need to get going. I've got training tomorrow morning," he throws a glance over to Ashley, who rolls her eyes. Something's going on here.

After he leaves, I look at Ashley in silence.

"What, Dad?" she asks impatiently. I offer her to come along with me to pick up the boys from their friends' houses, and she agrees. I know her well enough to know that it's better to wait a couple of minutes for her to cool off before talking about a touchy subject. After a couple of songs play on the radio, I turn the volume down and ask her what's going on with Jayden.

"His coach, that's what's going on. He's pressuring him to play against Columbus High, because if we lose this game, the season's pretty much over," she breaks into a well-re-hearsed monologue. "He checks in with the team doctor everyday about Jayden's ankle. He's constantly haranguing Jayden about playing next week, even though the doctor clearly says he needs two more weeks of rest. This is the type of injury that can become chronic if you don't let it heal right the first time. I read up on this type of injury. There are too many stories about athletes who ended their careers before they even began because of it."

I can hear the anxiety in her voice and try to ascertain what Jayden's view on this whole thing is. "He's not stupid, Dad. He knows he needs to look after himself. But the coach has been mentoring him for the past four years, he's like a second father. Do you know how hard it is for Jayden to say no to him?"

"Is Columbus High that good?" I try to remember who they even are, and if we've seen them play before. "I don't recall you mentioning them as direct rivals before. Why is Coach so insistent?"

"They're not that good, but without Jayden, we could lose.

We've already lost three games since his injury, and everyone's really frustrated. It's not just Coach, the other players are losing their patience as well. They talk to him about it in training. I'm afraid he'll cave and try to please everyone."

## 16. CRITICAL PATH AND CRITICAL CHAIN

On my twentieth day at the DOT, an hour before I'm supposed to take the kids over to Karen and go for a nice weekend away with Sally, I arrive for a meeting at Chambers' office that has been scheduled since my first day in office. Naomi, the legal adviser, walks in as well. I'm hardly surprised. After all, as early as our first meeting, Chambers clearly expressed which department was handling the problems he wanted fixing.

Chambers' desk is clear, and his secretary is nowhere to be seen.

He looks at me inquisitively, and when he sees I'm not quite catching his drift, he says, "Well, what are you waiting for? Are you going to tell us?" he asks.

"Tell you what?" I ask with genuine bewilderment.

"You've been studying the material for three weeks. Do you have any insights about the problems we're having? Why do most of our projects end up falling behind schedule, and why do half of them end up in court? Do you have any leads?"

I try to think back to all the claim files I reviewed over the past weeks and the work meetings I sat in. Did anything come up that suggested a common problem? Or better yet, a common solution? I can't come up with anything, so I grasp at the only straw I have. "Not really. Regarding the legal issue, I can only assume that contractors are filing claims because it's beneficial to them. And regarding the delays—to the best of my knowledge, the last person who tried to tackle the subject, though from a different angle, was Dr. Eli Goldratt. Have you heard about him?"

"Isn't he the physicist who wrote about bottlenecks?" Naomi jumps in and surprises the both of us.

"How do *you* know about him?" Chambers is stunned.

"What do you think, lawyers don't have hobbies? I think I read him while on vacation in Vermont a couple of years ago. Something about a theory of constraints, right?"

I am impressed. The woman was reading professional literature outside the field of her expertise while on vacation.

I clear my throat and begin. "Two years ago, I took a course on critical chain, the method he invented. I even brought in Dr. Adam Silver, an expert in theory of constraints, to build a schedule using critical chain for the 612 project. As you know, relocating the high-voltage cable put a spoke in our wheel; but, perhaps more importantly, as I was trying to solve the problem, I met two different individuals who told me that critical chain does more harm than good." I tell them about my conversation with the wall contractor who explained to me that subcontractors aren't following the schedule because it disrupts the flow of their work, and about my conversation with the claimer, Randy White, who told me that not only does critical chain not fix the problem, it makes it worse.

"Randy White said that?" Chambers sounds impressed. "We meet him occasionally, but only as an adversary. He's the leading claimer for most large contractors in the country."

"An insufferable man," Naomi contributes her opinion, "but one has to admit, he's very good at what he does. He's responsible for my two most painful losses in court."

"He said critical chain only makes things worse, did he? He's either arrogant, or he simply knows something we don't. And if that's the case—maybe that's the lead we've been looking for." Chambers speaks slowly while stroking the top of his head, where his remaining hairs connect to his bald spot. "Tell me. Do you think he might be willing to talk to you and explain this further?"

\*\*\*

Three days later, we are gathered in the DOT's conference room.

Randy White had immediately agreed to meet with me. He seemed very happy to see me again, even happier to learn that I had switched sides, and happier still when I asked for his help.

"You don't say? The DOT actually want to listen? Learn from their mistakes? That's hard to believe. I meet them a couple of times a year, always during discussions when we are on opposite sides of a claim, but never—and I mean *never*—have I seen so much as an inkling of willingness on their part to listen. They're always busy coming up with contrived, far-fetched legal arguments which they then foolishly believe themselves. Instead of worrying about managing projects, they are too busing managing claims over projects. They always send clueless lawyers to represent them who don't know what they're talking about, instead of sending engineers who know their business. And because they are so clueless, they trip over their own feet time and time again. I always beat them, not because I'm such a smart guy, but because they always bring up legal arguments that exist purely in the realm of abstraction, while I talk about engineering and construction in the real world. If those bunch of cheats are willing to listen, they must really be down in the dumps. And if they're willing to listen to me, of all people, they must be desperate."

This candid monologue from the otherwise calculating cynic took me by surprise. I couldn't imagine this is how he felt toward them. I mean, toward us... Following such a grand speech, I was fully prepared for a resounding refusal, but to my surprise—he agreed without hesitation. "If the DOT want to learn, I'm more than happy to help," he said. Not only did he agree to talk to me, he even offered to speak with everybody at the office.

Thus, we are gathered three days later. Randy White is sitting at the head of the table of conference room three, surrounded by Chambers, Naomi Griffin, Greg Nader, Jill Sommers—Information Systems Manager—and three other young interns whose names I haven't picked up yet, from legal, engineering, and finance, respectively.

"So," Randy White opens this unusual meeting, "Eric Price tells me that you at the DOT are asking yourselves how you can manage your affairs better. Furthermore, he asks whether managing using critical chain can reduce schedule delays and subsequent claims filed by people like me..."

He pauses before he continues.

"Before we begin, you're certainly aware that I can't discuss any project or contractor with you, because that's a conflict of interest. So, everything I will tell you today, should you want to listen, will be anecdotes about hypothetical contractors and projects."

"Obviously," Naomi says, being the closest among those present to represent the law.

"But in fact," he disregards her comment, "perhaps it's best we start by talking about other matters. Let's start with project scheduling theory. Since I realize not everyone here is an engineer, let me give a practical example, one that doesn't require graphs or Gantt charts. Say we want to build a next ten-story office building to fit the whole DOT staff, whose offices are currently dispersed across several temporary structures, making it hard to work efficiently."

I look around to see if his sly jab at the DOT causes a reaction, but we're still just at the start and everyone still has their patience.

He smiles and continues, "First we lay the foundation, then the support beams which hold up the first floor, then its floor, the columns, walls, and ceiling, and then we repeat the process for the second floor, third floor, fourth floor, etc. But in fact, after we are done erecting the first-floor ceiling, we can work inside it, simultaneously. We can lay the plumbing, the water pipes, the electricity, and then lay the floor tiles over the pipes, the plaster on the walls, then the windows, door, and kitchenette, all the way until we have a finished office. All this can go on at the same time we continue putting up the columns, walls, and ceilings of the next floors. After we finish erecting the second-floor roof, we can start working inside it, as well. In other words, we can carry out a whole range of activities at the same time. On the other hand, some things can't be done simultaneously. For example, we can't erect the second-floor ceiling until we finished the first. This division into activities that can be carried out simultaneously and activities that can only be done after others are completed is the basis for project timing, and from that stems the most basic term we use—critical path. The critical path is the longest string of project activities with no gaps between them. It starts with the first action, that of laying the building's foundations, and ends with turning over the keys to the office building. In our example, it's easy to see that the critical path will include the activities of erecting the building's skeleton, floor after floor, and finally the interior work on the last floor, which we can only begin to work on after completing the rest of the floors. The critical path, then, is the longest path of activities that cannot be done simultaneously. In other words, if we complete these activities with perfect efficiency, one after the other, without stops or gaps, we can finish the building at the earliest possible date."

One of the young interns, Raji, raises his hand and, without waiting to be called upon, launches his question, "But if, say, the plumbing contractor on the floor before last, whose work isn't on the critical path, leaves the project for a month because he got a lucrative offer to work on another project, wouldn't that delay the project and change the critical path, at the same time?" Good question.

"That's correct," Randy answers. "The critical path could change as a result of any number of reasons, the most common being the one you just mentioned—lack of resources without which you cannot perform the activities on the critical path. That was the first thing Eli Goldratt added to the idea of critical path, which he called 'critical chain.' Usually, the critical chain is longer than the critical path because it considers the constraints stemming from lack of resources, which critical path ignores."

"If the critical chain is longer than the critical path, how could it be regarded as a better solution?" Raji asks again. I note to myself that he might be a bit impatient, but he's sharp.

Randy seems to be enjoying these interruptions and uses them to steer the conversation back on track. "The critical chain only *appears* to be longer. In fact, if we try to perform a string of actions without having the resources to do so, we won't be able to do it. So, critical chain forces us to make sure we have all the resources necessary, thus preventing us from planning a schedule according to a critical path which effectively cannot be executed."

He pauses for a moment to look around the table. This seems to be a technique of his. He takes long pauses, coaxing his audience to jump in with a question, then leveraging those questions to deliver his next point.

"The second thing Goldratt said was that the difference between planning and executing is of a statistical nature. Something we plan to finish in a week, in practice could sometimes take two weeks and sometimes three days. Consequently, when people are asked to commit to a timeframe for performing an action, they always state the longest reasonable time. Two weeks, in our case. What we get as a result is a self-fulfilling prophecy. That has two reasons, first, when you know you have two weeks to do a one-week job, you allow yourself to start a week late. Second, even if you do finish a week before the date you are committed to, whomever is supposed to carry out the subsequent activity is only planned to begin work a week later, so the week you helped skim off the schedule goes to waste. However, if something goes wrong and you finish after your deadline, the next person down the chain pushes his deadline forward. This way, you lose when luck is against you, but you don't win when luck is with you, either. Clearly, the consequence of an accumulation of a large number of minor delays is a major delay for the project.

"To solve that," he goes on, "Goldratt did a very simple thing. He cut the length of every activity in half and added a safety margin to the end of the project, as long as one-half of the accumulated lengths he cut. In other words, he cut the safety periods each participant sought to set aside for himself alone, and in their place inserted one, single, all-encompassing safety period, comprising the length of half of all the activities put together. He called it a 'buffer' and placed it at the end of the project's schedule. That had two immediate effects: the first was that people stopped wasting time—simply because their time was halved, and they now had none to waste. The second was that even in instances where a project faced unforeseeable delays, it still had a significant buffer that could absorb these delays within the schedule's timeframe."

Chambers interrupts. He has sat in silence so far, but by his question I see he hasn't missed a word Randy has said. "That sounds simple enough to work," he says slowly, "and to the best of my knowledge, it does work, but not every time. Can you elaborate on that? When does it work and when does it not work? And for what reasons?"

"Well," Randy says, "in hindsight, we see that Goldratt got some of the details wrong. The critical chain method assumes a random distribution of the planned duration of actions versus the duration in practice. This is true for machines on a production line, but not when managing a project. In reality, meeting an action's projected deadlines depends mainly on the intention of the person executing it. When keeping the schedule is important to that person, he invests the resources and attention necessary. But when it clashes with his interests, he doesn't meet the deadline, delivering excuses rather than results."

Now it's Chambers again. I can see by the fact he's asking two consecutive questions just how much he wants to hold on to Goldratt's solution as a basis for solving our problems. "We know that Goldratt's idea improved a lot of projects significantly, and that in the worlds of industry, his idea is considered to be the safest way to finish a project on time. We also know that in our world, of large infrastructure projects, it's hardly used, and of the times it has been used—it failed. What we don't know is why. Are there any adjustments or alterations we could make to Goldratt's idea that would make it work for us?"

"Well," Randy says, "to answers that question we need to understand the difference between industrial projects, which work well with Goldratt's solution, and construction projects, which don't. In a nutshell—the difference lies in the multitude of parties involved and their conflicts of interest. Industrial projects are often internal projects, managed primarily by a factory's development department, employing factory employees who cooperate with each other regularly. Construction projects, on the other hand, are executed by dozens of different parties assembled together for the sake of the project through a tangled web of dozens of contracts, and which scatter as soon as the project is done. Their collaboration is a one-off, lasting only as long as the duration of the specific project. Each of them has their own interests, which are more important to them than the interests of the project.

"To the economists among you," he says and gestures toward CFO Greg Nader, "the problem is very familiar. It's called the principal-agent problem[1] , and it describes situations in which an agent's best interests stand in contrast to the interests of the body that employs him. The case of multiple-participant projects is even more complicated since you, as the owner of the project, employ dozens of different agents, each in charge of a different aspect of the project, and each with their own interests which clash with those of the project. Multiple principal-agent problems create extremely complex conflicts of interest. Even without going into the mathematical theory, you can understand that this problem is not limited to the theory of constraints, but touches deeply on game theory, as well. But we'll talk about that in our next meeting."

I look over at Chambers and see a look of encouragement

---

1   The principal-agent problem describes a situation in which the best interest of the agent clashes with the best interest of his employer, thus potentially incentivizing the agent to make decisions for his own benefit against that of the institution which employs him. For example, when a manager receives a bonus for company gains, but is not penalized for company losses, he is incentivized to take risks, even if their trading expectancy for the company is negative (meaning that loss is more likely than gain) because the trading expectancy for his own gain is positive.

in his eyes. Finally, someone has defined the problem, and even hinted there might be a solution. His gratitude is clear when he says, "Mr. White, thank you for your time. If possible, we'd love to schedule a follow-up meeting for next week."

## 17. SOLVING JAYDEN'S DILEMMA

The boys are at Karen's tonight, but because Ashley is working a shift this evening, she'll spend the night at my place—meaning another night with Sally is out of the question. Meanwhile, I string together the closest thing to a family gathering I can; I'm meeting Danielle at Tom's Café, hoping that Ashley will find a couple of minutes to sit with us.

Even under the dimmed lights at Tom's, Danielle looks great. I arrive late to the café, and she is already sitting at a table talking to my daughter. "Spare me the excuses." She gives me a kiss on the cheek and turns back to Ashley, "Even working for the government hasn't taught your dad to arrive on time."

"You know, Aunt Danielle, he's always had trouble sticking to schedule. But you should feel important if he's invited you here."

I don't appreciate the insinuation—both insinuations, in fact—and drop my smile. "I hope I'm not interrupting your girl talk."

"As a matter of fact, you are. But I have to get back to the tables anyway, so you two catch up and I'll come by when I can," Ashley stands up and tightens her apron around her waist. "What would you like, sir?"

"I would like my daughter to learn some manners, and my little sister to respect her elders," I answer. "And a draft beer would be nice."

Ashley walks away and Danielle smiles to me. "For the

life of me, I don't know how you managed to raise such a great kid."

Ever since I left Ethan and the 612, my conversations with Danielle have been much more pleasant. Beforehand, I felt there was an impenetrable barrier between us—that besides being siblings, we were also adversaries. Now, however, we can speak freely, without worrying about hitting a nerve. She tells me about her growing workload, about managing increasingly complex projects, and bigger and bigger budgets. "I spent so long dreaming to get to where I am now. I worked so hard to get here, but now…" she pauses to sip her drink, allowing me to jump in and complete her sentence, "There's still something missing?"

"Yes."

"Maybe you just need to focus on what you have? You know, anyone can make a list of all the things they don't have in life. And if there's something I've learned over the past few years, it's to appreciate what I do have. I know that sounds like a cheap self-help book, but I swear it's true."

"Eric, there are some things you can know in your mind are true, but that's not enough. What's gonna happen in ten years? In twenty years? Will I still keep going into the office and coming home to an empty house?"

"Danielle, I may not say this enough, but I admire who you've become and the things you've achieved." I look in her eyes and don't let her break eye contact. "You can't say, or even feel, that everything you've accomplished in life is insignificant simply because you don't have a relationship. I'm in the same situation. And I've been down before, as well. Believe me, it doesn't do you any good."

She cracks a little smile, "According to what I've heard, we're not exactly in the same situation."

What, did Ashley tell her already?

"I don't know what you think you understood, but you're drawing your own conclusions here."

"Okay, okay, relax…" she smiles again, "I'm glad at least one of us is making progress in that department."

"I take it Ashley spilled the beans about me the second you walked in."

"Wrong, again. Ashley and I talk regardless of you. I told you, I don't know how you managed to raise such a great kid. Here, look at her."

Ashley came up to our table without a tray, holding a cup of coffee. She sat down, placed the cup in front of her and added a pack of artificial sweetener. "I see by your silence that you were talking about me," she laughed and sipped her coffee.

"What else would we talk about?" Danielle said and looked at Ashley. They burst out laughing like a couple of 12-year-old girls. This evening, it was Danielle who looked more like a teenager.

"Dad, do you have plans for the weekend? I want Jayden to meet Danielle."

"It's about time I met the groom, don't you think?" Danielle couldn't help herself.

"But you have a game on Sunday, don't you? Columbus High are coming, if I remember correctly?"

"What, you didn't tell him?" Danielle turns to Ashley.

I'm no longer following. "Tell me what?"

"Jayden's not going to play on Sunday."

"Great. I'm glad you managed to convince him."

"Eric, you have no idea the lengths your daughter went to in order to make that happen."

"I'm assuming she visited you, and you gave her tips on how to talk to him. Something like that?"

"Absolutely not. I mean, she did come visit me, but she came up with the whole thing by herself, and that's much more difficult."

As it turns out, it really was more complicated than that. Ashley had spent several days worrying that Jayden would play on Sunday against his doctor's advice and put his career at risk. She approached his coach, but he explained that Columbus High are a completely different team now, comparing to the one they beat at the start of the season, thanks to Eddie Simmons—their star player who missed the first half of the season through injury. This time, he's going to play. And if Jayden sits this one out, Greenfield doesn't stand much of a chance. The coach admitted to her that he understands this could put Jayden at risk, but he thinks it'll be okay. She tried to protest, she even told the coach, "It'll be on your head, you'll never forgive yourself if he gets injured—" but to no avail. Right before Jayden and the rest of the team left the locker-room, she went back up to the stands and waited for him, as if nothing had happened.

Later, Ashley went over to Danielle and told her all about the situation. When my sister heard it was Columbus High, she told Ashley that a friend of hers, a woman she had once met at an engineering conference in Ohio, has a daughter about the same age that goes to that high school. Things gathered pace from that moment on, and after a series of phone calls and correspondences, it turned out that Eddie Simmons, Columbus High's star player, who had also just recovered from an injury—albeit a knee injury and not an ankle injury—still hasn't fully recovered. Furthermore, it turned out that he, like Jayden, was being pressured to play to help keep the team's season alive.

"And then, what did your daughter do?" Danielle asked excitedly. "Well? Go on, tell him!" Ashley was a little embarrassed, so my sister took the reins. "You know the French expression, *cherchez la femme*? Of course you do, 'look for the woman.' Ashley looked for and found Eddie Simmons' girlfriend who, as it turns out, felt exactly the same as her, and proposed an idea, they would agree in advance that both players won't play, thus putting themselves out of harm's way, and inform the coaches of their decision."

"Okay," I jump in, "that's really nice. But why would the coaches agree to that, or even believe it?"

"Let your daughter explain," Danielle takes another sip and passes the ball over to Ashley, who doesn't waste a second. "Put yourself in their position. Neither coach wants to screw up his star player's leg, and the only reason they're willing to take that risk is because they're convinced that that's what the other coach is going to do. Each of them thought that he had no choice, and that since the other coach is going to play his injured star player, he would have to do the same to stand a chance of winning. They thought their arms had been twisted. As soon as I went to Greenfield's coach and Amanda went to Columbus High's coach, and we told them about the agreement, they both pounced on the opportunity. It was agreed that both teams would try to win, but each would play without its injured star player. What do you say to that?"

Honestly? I'm very impressed. I would never have thought about that myself, and certainly wouldn't have tried to procure phone numbers and addresses of high school seniors halfway across the country.

"Wow," I say, "that's an absolutely brilliant solution. How did you come up with that?"

"You wouldn't believe me if I told you," my ingenious daughter replies. I can see the spark in her eyes. "I learned it in school. Only, I can't explain right now because it looks like the customers at table seventeen are about to send a convoy into the kitchen to see why they still haven't gotten their pizzas."

## 18. GAME THEORY AND THE PRISONER'S DILEMMA

"I'm really glad we're doing this," I say, visibly excited and a little nervous. In the meantime, I organize, for the third time, the bowls of (vegan!) snacks and glasses of juice. I check my phone again in case I missed a message in the minute since I last checked.

"Dad, it's just a rehearsal for my presentation, let's not make a big deal out of it." Ashley insists on staying grounded, but even she understands this is a big deal for me. Sally is going to meet the family, this time when everyone has their clothes on...

Believe it or not, this was all Ashley's idea. She has to deliver a presentation in economics class the day after tomorrow, and she was afraid I wouldn't be sufficiently critical and inquisitive, that her brothers would be bored, and that Danielle would only say positive things, no matter what. "Maybe we could invite Sally to my rehearsal?" she suggested the other day. "You said she was a doctor at a university, right? So she must know about game theory."

I was too taken aback to comprehend what she was talking about exactly; I didn't stop to think if Sally might actually know anything about game theory. But this opportunity was too good to pass up, so I immediately agreed, I said it was an excellent idea and that Sally would give her all the feedback she could possibly want.

Sally liked the idea, too. Instead of the routine introductory scenario where everyone is desperately trying to overcome the awkwardness through monotonous small talk, Ashley's presentation is a chance to break the ice in a field Sally is confident in. She didn't study economics, but she has a basic grasp of game theory from various conferences and guest lectures, which she assumed would suffice for high school level.

At eight-thirty sharp, the doorbell rings and I practically run to get to the door. I stand confused before the sight in front of me—Sally and Danielle, previously each belonging to a different thread of the story, standing together at my doorstep.

"I've already had the chance to meet your sister," Sally says as she leans in to kiss my cheek. Danielle smiles and gives me a thumbs-up to say that, so far, the introduction has been a success.

"Where's my favorite niece?" Danielle walks in and receives an enthusiastic hug from Ashley. "Are you ready to wow me again?"

Sally and I follow her in, and my daughter lets go of her aunt. "Hello, Sally," she says, and reaches out for a polite handshake with a friendly smile.

So far, so good.

The boys come downstairs from their room, say hello politely to Sally, and join us in the living room. If I'm being honest, they're here with us more because I promised we'd have pizza when Ashley's finished than due to any spontaneous fascination with game theory.

"Okay, shall we start?" I say when everyone's sat down. Ashley stands before the large whiteboard I got on the way back at Walmart, which is now leaning against the large wall in the living room.

She writes down in big bold letters, "The Prisoner's Dilemma."

I've heard about the prisoner's dilemma several times. If hard-pressed, I could probably give a general outline, but no more than that. So, I listen intently as Ashley begins to talk.

"Two suspects were caught fleeing the scene of an armed robbery, but the police have no evidence or witnesses to tie them to the crime," she opens. "After several hours at the station, while they are being interrogated separately in different rooms, the precinct chief decides to pose a bargain, and he offers each one of them separately to incriminate the other and he tells each of them that if the two of them remain silent, they will be accused of vagrancy and resisting arrest, and will each be punished with one year in jail. If one of them remains silent but the other incriminates him, the silent one will get fifteen years in jail while the rat will go free. If both prisoners incriminate each other, they will each be punished with five years in prison."

"Can cops even do that??" Josh jumps in protest. "Yeah," Ben joins in, "that's not fair. They're not judges!"

"Boys, it's just a theoretical discussion," Danielle intervenes. Following their confused expressions, she adds, "it's just a made-up example we use as an exercise, kay?"

"Go on, Ashley," Sally says after the boys settle down. "So far, you're doing great."

"Okay, so now I ask you, the students, which would you choose? To incriminate your colleague or keep silent?"

"I already know the answer," Sally says as she gets up from

the couch, "so in the meantime, I'll fix everyone something to drink. How about herbal tea?" Danielle and I sneak a smile at each other, and answer that we'd love a coffee. "Just try it, what do you have to lose? I have hibiscus flower essence in my purse. You'll love it. I promise." She disappears into the kitchen, while we sit in front of Ashley and think.

"You know what; let's see for real," Ashley rips a couple of pages from her notebook, cuts them in half, and hands each of us half a sheet of paper.

"Remember, you're looking to get the best results for yourselves alone. We're not talking about siblings, or people you'd be willing to go to jail for. Okay? Let's try. Dad—you're playing against Danielle. Ben, you're playing against Josh. Take a minute," she hands us pens. A couple of moments later, I manage to retrieve the correct answer from the back of my mind, and write down, INCRIMINATE. I look over at Danielle, who's also jotting something down on her sheet of paper, while the two kids struggle to come to a decision. A minute later, Josh says in exasperation, "It's impossible to answer, because I can't know in advance what Ben will do." Ben follows suit, complaining the riddle is stupid.

"It's true, you can't know what the other person will do," I say, "but despite that, you can say that either way, if I incriminate the other person, I get a better result. If Danielle chooses to incriminate me as well, I get five years in prison instead of fifteen if I had kept silent. If Danielle chooses to keep silent, then I get to go free, instead of spending a year in prison if I had kept silent too. It's better to be a rat. No question about it."

I look over at Danielle and guess what she wrote down. If

I know my sister, she wrote the same thing as me.

"Let's see," Ashley says theatrically as she looks at the folded sheets of paper we hand her. "Dad, Aunt Danielle, I'm very sorry, but you're both going to jail for five years! Wanna try again?"

"No, the same thing is going to happen again, isn't it?" Danielle is quick to grasp the situation. "We didn't make a mistake. We reached the best outcome under the rules you defined. Under these circumstances, incriminating the other is the rational choice, so we'll both choose it again next time and end up with a five-year sentence again."

"But if we could have collaborated, we would have ended up with only a one-year sentence," I support the example.

"Good job, children," Ashley says with a smile, while Sally walks in with a steaming, odd-smelling pitcher of tea. "And that's what the prisoner's dilemma teaches us, bad rules make for bad consequences."

"You mean, it will always lead to a worse outcome than could otherwise have been obtained?" I ask Ashley, trying to ascertain her understanding of the issue.

"Precisely."

"And is there a solution to prevent the bad outcome?"

"Actually, there is a solution to the prisoner's dilemma," Ashley says, and suddenly doesn't look as confident as before. "But I have to admit, I don't exactly understand it."

Naturally, we all turn to look at Sally. "The tea's really good," she teases us. I'm shocked to see just how quickly she's settled in.

"Come on, Sally," Ashley urges her, "you must know something about it, right?"

"You mean the iterated prisoner's dilemma?"

"Yes. That's the solution I saw in the textbook and on the internet, but I didn't really understand how it solves the problem."

"It doesn't solve the problem, it reconfigures its rules," Sally says. Danielle and I both look at her inquisitively. "I'll give you an example. Your father, for example, worked with subcontractors in all of his projects."

I nod in support of the example, and she continues.

"Some of them do jobs like laying underground pipes and cables. Since they immediately cover their work in soil, they could use substandard materials and save quite a lot of money, with hardly any chance of anyone ever knowing. And yet, they don't do it. Can you guess why?"

"Because my dad employs only honest subcontractors," Ashley boasts. "And besides, they're probably scared that if Dad ever caught them, he'd never work with them again."

"That's right," Sally says. "Can you explain how that influences their decision-making?"

"I think that it makes so that in the long-run, the profit that they might make by using cheaper materials is offset by the prospect of losing future work," Ashely says.

"Exactly. And that, Ashley, is an example of the iterated prisoner's dilemma—when the same players expect to meet again and again, their strategy changes because they take into account not only immediate gain but all future losses as well."

Across the couch, I can see Danielle smiling and nodding, perhaps impressed by the new insight, perhaps impressed by her brother's new girlfriend. Perhaps both.

"I think I get it now," Ashley turns to Sally, "in both cases the prisoner is trying to maximize his own personal gain, but the potential for personal gain changes when the rules change."

"Good job. That is both accurate and precise," Sally says. I think I see something resembling maternal pride in her expression. "And that's what leads us to the final point, which turns the prisoner's dilemma from an interesting riddle to one of the most powerful tools in the world. You can call it 'the Manager's Dilemma.' While the prisoner's dilemma shows us how bad rules make for bad outcomes, the manager's dilemma is about how to make good rules. Rules that will make all of the manager's employees make good decisions. In an organization where an employee stands to suffer personal loss by making decisions which are good for the organization, he would prefer to make not-so-good decisions, but ones that won't hurt him personally. In such an organization, the manager would have to intervene again and again to correct his employees' decisions. On the other hand, if he manages to create a better framework in which employees are personally rewarded for making decisions for the good of the organization, then management becomes easier, because it is in everyone's best interest to pull the cart in the same direction. The direction of the good of the organization. In such a situation, the manager doesn't need to intervene in his employees' decisions, because he knows their decisions will be beneficial to the company just as they will be beneficial for them personally."

"But how could I explain that in the presentation?"

"Tell them what you did for Jayden with Amanda's help,"

I tell her. "How you managed to change the framework in which both coaches made their decisions."

"I'm sure you'll do great, sweetie," Sally concludes. This is the second time she's called her that, and to everyone sitting in the living room, it sounds perfectly natural.

## 19. WHY IS A GOAL FUNCTION NECESSARY?

"What are you so pleased about?" a friendly pat that nearly breaks my shoulder accompanies the deep, low voice behind me. I don't need to turn around to know who it is.

"Hi Randy," I try to sound as ordinary as I can, "how are you?"

"I'm great, thanks. I'm glad to see the place is still standing," he chuckles as I turn to face him.

"Are you sure you're glad? I don't think you'd mind it if the whole place burned down." Chambers, who joins us, picks up the conversation, "You don't exactly love this office, do you?"

"On the contrary," Randy smiles, "we're business partners, aren't we? Every time I want to buy a new car or go on vacation, I check to see what projects you're working on, and call the general contractor."

No one speaks to Chambers that way, but somehow Randy pulls it off. The big boss smiles and takes Randy's jabs to the chin. Those who know him know that that's the clearest indication of the respect he has for Randy.

"So, in order for you to stop robbing us, we've invited you to install a better lock for us. Would you say that metaphor is about right?

"Not really," Randy replies, "your lawyers are trying to install locks and defenses against every possible claim. I'm just here to show you why they can't do it—because no such locks exist. The only way to stop the robbers from cleaning you out is to change their motivation."

He stops and glances at his watch, as if to say, *enough messing around, we're here to work.*

When we are all sat in the conference room, Chambers lifts two hands in the air and the chatting quiets down to a low murmur. Chambers thanks Randy for the meetings and recounts where we left off, "As you may remember, last time we met we spoke about Goldratt's solution—cutting down to half the length of all activities and adding half of what we cut to the end as a buffer. The buffer allows us to complete the project on time, even in cases where Murphy strikes, and even when he strikes hard. We finished with Mr. White giving us a little teaser for today's meeting, promising to explain the matter of conflicts of interest between all parties working on the project, and to enlighten us about how to resolve it."

He finishes his introduction with an appeal to all of us, "This is what we asked Randy to try and explain to us today. Keep an open mind and pay close attention. You may receive the most important professional insight of your life today," he pauses for a moment and adds, "and if I know Randy White, it's going to be among the most frustrating ones, as well."

Randy stands up. Without him uttering even a single word, his charisma is undeniable, all eyes are set on him, his flamboyant clothes, his large frame, and his very particular smile—treading the thin line between confidence and arrogance.

When he starts talking, his low bass voice resonates in the room, as if it were amplified by five microphones set in front of him.

"Hello, everyone." He starts by teasing, "We don't have much time today, because I have a lot of claims to prepare and you have a lot of meetings to attend and coffee to drink, so let's get right down to it." He lets the spontaneous bursts of laughter in the audience die down, and continues. "Before we start, I want to tell you about a vacation I took two years ago, okay?"

I look over at Chambers. By the look on his face, he has no idea what Randy is up to, either.

"So, two years ago, when Carry, my daughter, graduated college, she decided there would be nothing cooler than inviting her dad to travel around the world with her. Let me tell you—I wasn't sure if I should be proud that she chose me to accompany her, or disappointed that she still needs her daddy around at that stage in life."

The audience laughs and exchanges glances, as if to say, *where did they find this piece of work?*

Randy continues, "Of all the places in the world, she chose Nepal. I told her, if you're looking for dirt and bad infrastructure, she could've just gone to Oklahoma and save my money, but she wouldn't listen. Long story short, a month later, after two days of excruciating connection flights, we found ourselves in Katmandu. Since it was already evening, and we had just suffered through two days of airplane food, we walked into a restaurant recommended on TripAdvisor. The place was packed, so they sat us down at a table with some Australian travelers. Yes, none of that 'wait for a table' or 'sit at the bar' crap. Believe me, it works great."

I look over at the employees in the audience and notice

that their level of attention is higher than what I'm used to seeing from them during our weekly meetings. I guess a claimer has to know how to tell a story.

"So, we're sitting with the young Australian travelers. I occasionally throw a mean look toward anyone staring a bit too long at Carry. A couple of beers later, we become friends. It turns out they can apparently climb as well as they can drink, and as one of them—who's on his sixth beer—tells us, they're planning to go *full Monty,* which is Australian-climber slang for climbing Mount Everest. At some point, one of them pulls out a map. What are you looking at me for, that's what you do when you don't have wi-fi everywhere! I hope some of you still work with real maps, and not just whatever pops up on your tablets and smartphones."

I'm sure Randy worked on this bit at home, that it's his way of keeping everyone alert. It's working.

"So, one of the kangaroos pulls out a map and spreads it across the table. Carry is excited and stands up to get a better look. But I'm in the middle of my steak, and with all due respect to Mount Everest, you know..." he pats his formidable belly with the palm of his hand. "They start showing Carry the trail, and even from across the table, I can see it goes up and down several ridges and valleys before reaching the Everest summit. One of them explains to me that that's the shortest possible route, and that it really does have an inexhaustible number of ascents and descents. Carry remarks that they probably have to climb much further than the actual elevation of the summit, and one of them decides to do the math. We went over section by section, and it turned out that while the summit is three-miles higher than the starting point, the trail they intended to take amounts to a seven-mile climb—more than double!"

Randy pauses for dramatic effect, emphasizing that what he just said was particularly important.

"You understand why that is, right?" he asks. Everyone seems to understand.

"Good. So, why did I tell you this story?"

I was asking myself the same question.

"Because at that moment, despite the beer and the jubilance, I realized something very important about Eli Goldratt's theory."

Chambers sits up in his chair, and, like most people in the room, seems skeptical.

"Those of you who read *The Goal* probably remember that what Goldratt built in the end was a process of constant improvement based on five steps repeated again and again. Each round is intended to remove another constraint which stands between us and better performance. Through this method, which he called the *five focusing steps*, he argued that we can achieve a process of constant improvement. At that moment in Nepal, though, I realized that even if the process he describes is true, it can't possibly be enough. When you want to climb from Lhasa to Everest—you can't go from start to finish simply by improving your position—that is, by constantly climbing up. To reach the summit, you need to identify it, plot a course to reach it, and stick to the plan the whole way through. Following such a trail, you find yourself occasionally climbing ridges and occasionally descending into valleys but, either way, are always getting closer and closer to the summit of Mount Everest."

"You see," he raises his voice and looks around the room with a steely gaze, "only when you see the entire path do you realize that a certain decrease in altitude is in fact an improvement which gets you closer to the summit. So long as we try to improve ourselves strictly in terms of altitude, the best we can reach is the top of the particular hill we are currently standing on. This hill could be a tiny ten-foot mound for all practical matters, but once we are standing on its slope, the best we can reach by constant improvement is the top of it. And a ten-foot hill, ladies and gentlemen, is not our target! If there is a valley between us and the summit—or, like in real life, several huge valleys—we will never reach the summit by simply climbing up from one elevation line to the next. In other words, Goldratt's five focusing steps provide a process of improvement *only in context of the current solution*. In the case of the Australian travelers, that kind of improvement would be climbing farther up the hill they are already standing on. To go higher than the top of that hill, you need a new solution. You need to expand the frame of reference from the current hill to the entire Himalayan mass. Only when you see the entire trail on the map can you truly appreciate that descending the hill serves the purpose of going higher, bringing us closer to Mount Everest. As long as we focus solely on improving our present situation, we can never go any higher than the top of the hill we are standing on."

Randy pauses for a moment and scans the room, trying to ascertain if the audience follows his trail of thought and understands the importance of what he just said. Seeing more than one confused face in front of him, Randy assumes the message hasn't been understood, so he repeats, "What I understood that day in the restaurant was that the process of constant improvement can only lead to local optimization. But then, the apple hit my head. Goldratt taught us to replace local optimization with global optimization, so how could the five focusing steps lead in the exact opposite direction? For the whole week that followed, during every break along the trail, and at night in the inns along the way, Carry and I were glued to our Kindles, rereading over and over again what Goldratt wrote about transitioning from local to global optimization. Seven days of grueling ascents and descents later, both our feet and our minds ached, but we cracked it.

"When you look at what Goldratt did, and not just what he said, you notice he didn't use only the five steps, but two other steps, as well. The first step was expanding the frame of reference. This is the frame for which he sought global optimization. At first, he expanded the frame from one man-ufacturing department to a factory in its entirety. Then, he expanded from the factory to the corporation, which needs to sell the products the factory makes, and then to the entire supply chain, which supplies and sells raw materials and parts to the corporation. In the second step, he determined the target you need to aim for in order to achieve global optimization. His definition was that the target is 'to ensure maximum profitability, now and in the future.'

"Goldratt himself never bothered to define the first two steps," he went on, "probably because they seemed to him to be obvious. The problem with critical chain began when Goldratt started dealing with project management and was still unfledged in the field. His intuition regarding the field was still undeveloped, leading him to define his frame of reference inaccurately, and, subsequently, to define an inaccurate target for it, finishing projects according to their schedule."

"That seems accurate enough for me," Chambers jumps in. "I'd gladly settle for finishing our projects on time. That would be a tremendous success."

Randy looks at Chambers, pauses for a moment, and decides to continue without replying.

"You'll see in a minute that the most important thing is to begin with an accurate definition of the frame of reference, the frame for which you seek global optimization. When Goldratt invented the critical chain, he viewed the project through the lens of the contractor. Those who followed him tried to view projects through the lens of the client. They didn't realize that those were two completely different frames of reference, that the increased value for each of them is completely different."

"Why?" Chambers interjects, "A good project is a good project, whether you're a contractor or a client or a designer."

"That is, of course, completely wrong," Randy looks at Chambers and continues explaining. "For the contractor, the project framework includes his own work and that of his subcontractors. For the client, however, the project framework includes not only that, but also the work of all the different designers, the project manager, the different bodies who have extant infrastructure that needs to be relocated for the project, the owners of the land that needs to be expropriated for the project, etc. While the contractor maximizes the value of *his project* by filing claims which increase his earnings, those same claims diminish the value for the client; while the contractor maximizes the value of the project by saving on expenses, the client is completely indifferent to those savings. While a prompt conclusion of the project and early use of the road significantly increases the value of the project for the client, that value is much less significant for the contractor, and is sometimes even negative." He looks at Chambers again and says, "Whichever lens you choose to look through, a good project for the client and a good project for the contractor are two completely different things."

"Why is that important?" Greg Nader asks. "What do we care what the contractor thinks? We define *our* project to him, and he needs to accommodate us."

"I'll get to that in a minute," Randy goes on, "what's important to see here is that the error in defining the frame of reference led to another error, the error in defining the goal. Two such disparate frames of reference cannot share the same goal."

He stops and scans the room again, and again it seems like the message did not get through. The first one to crack is Chambers, who is desperate not to finish the meeting without receiving applicable insight. He breaks the silence by saying to Randy in a dry voice, "Mr. White, the younger guys here might be sharper than me, but I have to admit I don't see how the problems of mountain climbers in the Himalayas relate to road construction and project management in the United States of America."

The rustle of people moving uncomfortably in their chairs, without another word being said, suggests that Chambers is not the only one to feel this way. But Randy White is unimpressed. On the contrary. "I'm sorry, Mr. Chambers," he says, "I'm sorry if I was unclear. The connection is the road leading to Mount Everest. Or in other words, the connection is—how to gauge progress. The question is, then, when you gauge the progress of your projects—do you measure how many elevation lines you've ascended, or do you measure miles along the trail?"

Finally, someone raises his hand. It's Raji again, the young upstart from last week's meeting. He doesn't wait for Randy to call on him, and blurts, "We're not stupid. Of course we don't measure elevation lines. We measure progress along the project's critical path. That's the equivalent of measuring miles along the trail to Mount Everest."

"*Bravo!*" Randy White practically shouts. "The critical path is the equivalent of measuring miles along the trail to Mount Everest." He shifts his gaze from one member of the audience to another, and repeats the sentence, slowly, emphasizing every word, "*The – critical – path – is – the – equivalent – of – measuring – miles – along – the – trail – to – Mount – Everest.*"

And then, in a perfect theatrical reversal, he suddenly feigns a look of embarrassment, fixes his gaze on Raji, and asks him in his thunderous voice, "Is that so? Is the critical path the equivalent of measuring miles along the trail to the summit?" When no one offers a response, he continues with, "If the critical path was indeed equivalent to the trail to the summit, then reaching its end on schedule would be equivalent to conquering Mount Everest, and the project would be labeled a success. But in reality, everyone knows that's not the case. If you open the basic manual for project management, you'll find that the project manager's objective is to meet the project's schedule, budget, scope, and quality goals. The critical path gauges only one of those four criteria—the project's schedule objective. In other words, it very well may be that our progress along the critical path is coming along great, but in reality, we are on course to finishing on schedule a project with a bloated budget, reduced content, and such inferior quality that it'll probably collapse in a year or two."

Raji seizes Randy's pause and barges in again, "But that's exactly why Goldratt substituted the critical path with the critical chain."

Even he feels, as he finishes his sentence, that it doesn't stand on firm ground, as evidenced by the fact he doesn't complete his thought, and his words remain suspended in the air of the cramped conference room. The room falls silent, and I can see uncertain gazes darting back and forth from Raji to Randy.

Randy White is not the type of man to pass on rhetoric. He raises his hand in the air to get everyone's attention again, and slowly delivers his punchline, "Essentially, the critical chain is no different than the critical path. Neither of the paths scrutinize nor try to improve the value of the project as a whole. They both turn the same blind eye to cost, scope of work, and quality, focusing exclusively on the project's duration. In other words, if increasing the project's value to its fullest limit is our equivalent of walking the trail all the way up to Mount Everest, then using critical path or critical chain are two surefire ways to get us, at best, to the top of the hill we are standing on."

After dropping this bombshell, he takes a break and slowly

pours himself a cup of water from the bottle on the table in front of him.

I feel the ground slipping underneath my feet. What he just said means that in all my attempts to find an effective way to apply critical chain for road construction projects, I was simply heading down a blind alley. In one fell swoop, Randy had sent me back to square one, to my first day at the DOT, when Chambers assigned me the task of finding an all-encompassing solution to his problems.

It seems I'm not the only one to feel this way, as Chambers himself is the first to break the tense silence in the room. Clearly upset at what he just heard, he slowly talks through clenched teeth, "If what you're saying is true, then the critical chain is completely useless. Don't the thousands of projects that concluded on schedule prove you wrong? I remind you that global statistics indicate that about eighty-five percent of all projects finish with delays and only about twenty percent finish on time, while critical chain boasts a far better ratio."

I remind myself that Chambers gambled on critical chain no less than I did, and that he, no less than me, is very reluctant to discover that he bet on the wrong horse.

Randy tinkers with the bottle, pours some water, and examines it by holding up the glass to the florescent lights as if it were nothing short of the finest red wine. After he slowly sips his drink, he can see we are glued to the edges of our seats in suspense, so he finally answers.

"You can relax," he tells us. "As you already know, I am not one to deny what is plain for all to see. The thousands of projects that have ended on schedule do indeed prove that the critical chain has been very beneficial. The problem is, very few among those thousands of projects were in our field. And furthermore—most attempts to apply critical chain in our field have yielded zero positive results. I'm not against critical chain; on the contrary, I think it contains two fantastic ideas. All I've said was that you can't use it to climb Mount Everest, since it is inherently designed to lead you to the top of the hill you are already standing on."

I can see Chambers deliberating whether to simply accept Randy's point, and I decide to beat him to it. "Can you define precisely what those two fantastic ideas are?" I ask him.

"Sure," he answers. "The first is that there are two types of connections between the project's activities, not one, not just the order of execution, but the order of resources, as well. The second idea is that you need to decrease the buffers between different activities and add one large buffer at the end of the project, instead. These two ideas are so simple and obvious that right after you hear them you think to yourself, *how did no one think of them before?* But the fact is until Goldratt came along, no one had thought of them."

"That's it?" I ask. "That's all critical chain boils down to in your opinion? What about the idea of buffers for chains that feed the critical chain? What about the idea that you should delay starting activities until the last possible moment, in order to advance the project and ensure it finishes on time? And what about the idea that you should hold back resources that are necessary for work on critical activities so that they'll be available as soon as work starts?"

Randy takes a long, hard look at me, and pours the second bucket of ice water of the day over my head. "All those ideas are nice in theory, but when you apply them in our field, they in fact prevent thousands of projects from finishing on time," he says in a low voice. Before I can get a word in, he continues, "The problem is that the only way to understand why those ideas are wrong is to follow the trail to the Everest that we walked together today."

At this point in the conversation, everyone is exhausted. It seems I'm not the only one Randy has put into intellectual vertigo. The finance and legal people seem to have lost all interest; the only reason they are still in the room is out of politeness. I don't blame them. This is quite far removed from their expertise, and the feeling that they don't follow Randy's logic doesn't bruise their professional ego. For the engineering people, the opposite is true, both the senior employees, like myself and Chambers, and the younger employees, like Raji and Linda and Marissa, came into the conference room as experts in their field, and now Randy White tells us that half of what we know about our profession is inherently false. On top of that, it doesn't seem like he's about to propose an alternative.

The first person to finally lose his cool is, once again, the big boss, Martin Chambers. "So, what's the bottom line?" he practically shouts. All eyes turn to him. Again, I relate to his plight and his burning desire to see this matter resolved. "If the critical chain can't help, then what can?"

Randy keeps his cool, smiles at Chambers but addresses the whole room. "What I'm suggesting is that you redefine your goal. It's not going to be easy, but, since I've walked this path before, I can promise you it ends well. You can run projects efficiently. You can finish them on time, on budget, and without claims. What this requires of you is to properly define your goal."

He stops, glances at his watch, and says, "I think our meeting is done. Let's meet again, same place, same time, next week. Your homework is to come with a clear definition of your goal. I will accompany you from that point on."

Raji refuses to accept that the meeting is adjourned. "Can you give us any guidelines on how to approach the question?" he asks Randy, and I understand he's up for the challenge.

"Of course. What you need to find is a way to define your goal in a clear manner. As clear as the summit of Mount Everest. In fact, the definition of your goal should be so clear and simple that anyone working on the project could use it. Every time they deliberate between two alternatives, they could make that decision based on what best promotes the goal, based on the question, does this alternative promote or detract from the goal?"

*Define your goal clearly.* The sentence repeats in my mind as I pack my things and head home.

# 20. UNLOCKING THE GOAL FUNCTION

Raji Umair graduated with honors from engineering school eighteen months ago, and the DOT is his first job. He's less than half the average age of the rest of the DOT employees. A combination of high intelligence and an opinionated mind, a foreign accent, zero experience in real-world engineering, and an environment in which everyone knows better than him makes the DOT a difficult place for him. His studies were funded by the DOT as part of an extended program to develop a reserve of skilled managers; in return, Raji has to work at the DOT for a period of time equal to that of his studies. The problem is that due to his inexperience, there is no position he is actually qualified to fill, so he's found himself drifting from one assistant job to the other, leaving no impression and being of very little use. I've come across him a couple of times in the corridors of the DOT, and recently during our meetings with Randy White. On the one hand, I couldn't avoid the feeling that his brash, and unfounded opinions are quite annoying. On the other hand, I can't help but be reminded of another young man I met twenty odd years ago who was much the same: me.

Before everyone dispersed at the end of the meeting, I asked Raji if wanted to help me try and figure out an answer to Randy's homework assignment. He was stunned for two reasons—one, I had sought to consult him; two, I appointed our meeting for Monday at 6 a.m., a full three hours before the phones start ringing and the workday starts. By the look on his face, I can see that the very existence of 6 a.m. is something he has heard rumors about but never seen for himself.

It's still dark out when we arrive, almost in perfect synchronicity, at the parking lot of the DOT. After pouring two strong cups of coffee, we settle in at my office, close the door, and try to solve Randy's riddle.

"Let's start with what Randy said," I propose, "let's map what we know of other projects' goals and try to work back toward a more generalized goal."

He nods in agreement. I get up and go to the whiteboard hung on a wall in my office, grab a black marker and write a header: 'Project Goals.'

Underneath it, I write in four short lines:

"Stay on budget."

"Finish on time."

"Meet quality objectives."

"Execute full scope."

I pause for a moment, look at the board, and ask Raji, "Do you agree with this for a start?"

"I think so," he says, "but remember—Randy says there should be only one target. That means all of these clauses should be united into a more general goal."

"I remember. He also said that the goal should be defined in a way that could be used to help choose between alternatives. I think that means the goal should be stated in numbers—so we can see if the number increases or decreases as we make changes. If it increases, we are getting closer to our goal, and if it decreases, then we are straying from it. I understand how you can express budgetary goals in numbers, perhaps even schedule goals—but quality and scope, those are not quantifiable. What do we do with them?"

We try to come up with numerical relations between the non-quantifiable goals—quality and scope—and tie them together. But so far, our efforts amount to nothing.

The DOT quality measures are the kind that seem like a good idea but are ultimately inapplicable. At the end of every project, the department managers always gather for a final meeting in which they grade the contractor's performance vis-à-vis ten different criteria which, aggregated, make up a final grade for the contractor's work on the project. Despite the orderly method, senior employees told me that final grades have never been applied in any meaningful way to future projects. The grade mounts to not much more than a reflection of the cordiality or animosity between the contractor and the different department managers. Furthermore, his performance is based on the quality of the design he works with, which, we all agree, he is not accountable for.

Regarding scope, we fare even worse. We can't find even a single way to express in numbers the value of the change in scope.

One hour and another cup of coffee later, I have to admit we've reached a dead-end, and I propose we try to find another way to look at the problem.

To avoid pulling rank and imposing my ideas on our brainstorming session, I propose Raji starts this time, that he defines how we should think about Randy's goal.

"Let's approach this like a logic puzzle," he says, looking at me warily to see if I am actually going to let him lead this process. "Let's try to define what information we have and what information we lack, to start with."

I nod to indicate I agree with his direction, and he steps up to the board. I notice he doesn't erase what I wrote, he's a low-level assistant and I'm the chief engineer after all. He draws a line down the board to separate what I wrote and starts writing in the empty space.

"One – need to define project goal."

"Two – definition should be quantitative and expressed in numbers."

"Three – it should allow everyone deliberating between two alternatives to arrive at the best solution."

So far, so good.

"I think," he says a bit hesitantly, "that the second clause indicates we're looking for a mathematical function."

"That's reasonable," I pick up his train of thought, "the problem is that it doesn't gel with the third clause, on the one hand, this function needs to encompass every single aspect of the project, otherwise it won't necessarily be applicable to any two alternatives. Such a function would be very complex. On the other hand, since the function should allow anyone to weight up their alternatives, it has to be simple enough for anyone to use. I don't see how those two things can sit together."

A long silence pervades the room. I read and reread what's written on the board, and Raji does the same. After a long, despairing minute, Raji says, "This might sound petty, but, since we're stuck, there's a slight inaccuracy in one of the clauses…"

"We've made no major breakthrough so far," I sense the agitation in my voice, "even something petty would be an improvement."

"Look," he says slowly, "this is probably nothing, but you see—Randy said we need to define *our* goals, and these don't look like *our* goals."

This does seem like a pretty flimsy lead, but we've got nothing else, so I decide to play the game.

"On my side of the board I put down four goals, but I think none of those are actually our goals or our projects' goals. They seem to me to be the project manager's goals. If he completes the project on budget, on time, with high quality and in full scope, he will be lauded by his employers."

"But isn't that a sign that the project achieved its goals?" I find his youthful naivety endearing. To explain the obvious, I say, "Maybe that's a sign that the designer planned the project with an inflated budget in the first place, which is why we didn't exceed it. Or maybe the amount of time allocated in the first place was too much, and that's why we managed to keep the schedule. Or perhaps the entire project is a product of some political whim, and never should have been authorized to begin with."

He is undeterred by my negativity. "What you're saying is that the purpose of the project is not to be finished on budget or on time, or with a certain quality or scope. So, what is its purpose?"

The hypothetical nature of the conversation is starting to get on my nerves, but, since I am the one who invited Raji and not the other way around, I keep my answers polite—though just barely.

"For god's sake, what do you mean what is its purpose?" I say, exasperated. "If it's a road construction project, it's purpose is to be driven on."

"So, maybe the project's goal function isn't about the road but about the people driving on the road?" You have to hand it to the guy, he may be irritating, but he doesn't give up easily. Or, maybe, those are actually the same thing.

"But how can you draw a connection between the driver's goal and alternatives for constructing the road?"

"You're right," he says in a pensive voice, "I suppose we're at a dead-end here too."

"Listen," I say in one final attempt for today, "the only function I know which concerns drivers is the function we use to decide which kind of road to construct. But I don't see how that could relate to our problems."

"What kind of function is it?" he asks.

"The simplest one you can think of. We calculate how much driving time will be saved if we construct the road, how many accidents will be prevented, how much air pollution would be avoided, and so forth, and each of those criteria is assigned a monetary value. We then conduct an engineering evaluation—how much it would cost to construct the road—and then we divide benefit by cost. The higher the result is, the more worthwhile it is to build the road. In theory, the roads we construct are the ones with the highest ratio.

"And that's it?"

"To keep it from being too simple, the finance people capitalize the whole thing so that the immediate gain would be considered greater than the same gains ten years down the line."

He listens attentively and says, "So we calculate the economic value of the road for the public. It's the IRR, the internal rate of return."[2]

I can now spot those honors he graduated with. "That's right," I answer. "In fact, it's the exact IRR equation they teach in Accounting 101, only we apply it to road construction. Problem is, I don't see any way to connect it to anything that's relevant to our situation."

"But if the project is more expensive, the IRR goes down?" he doesn't relent.

"Of course," I answer.

"So, if our goal function is the IRR, then perhaps we have our connection to keeping the project's budget."

Well, that's a moon shot.

"And what about time?" I ask. "How do you tie the need to finish a project on schedule with the IRR formula?"

He thinks for a minute and says, "When you calculate the internal rate of return, time is actually an important factor. I mean, what you're actually doing is calculating income and expenses per year and capitalizing it for today. Most of the project's expenses are concentrated in the beginning, and only after the project is done does it start to make money."

"Which means that the shorter the construction period, the shorter the period of interest on the investment…" I pick up his train of thought. "Which means, we have our connection between time and the goal function."

That's two out of four. This is no longer seems like a

---

2   Internal Rate of Return (IRR) is an index to assess the expediency of an investment. The higher the IRR, the more profitable the investment is projected to be; when the rate is negative, the investment is projected to run at a loss.

moon shot, but actually looks quite promising. I think for a moment and say, "I think there's even more to that than just reducing the cost of interest. The earlier we finish the road, the earlier it can be used. Since it never stops being used, not only does the return of investment being earlier, it lasts longer. A road constructed in one year will produce greater value than a road constructed in two years. So, not only does the return of investment begin *earlier*, it also *increases*."

"And what about quality?" he asks. "How does that tie into the goal function?" We throw around some ideas for a couple of minutes before reaching the conclusion that the higher the quality of the project, the less expenses you will later incur through repairs and maintenance, which of course influences the value of the goal function.

"Only one left," he says. "How does scope relate to all of this?"

"That's simple. Every part of the project's scope contributes something to its value, otherwise we wouldn't have planned it in the first place. Therefore, if we don't execute part of the plan, we decrease the project's cost on the one hand, but decrease its value to consumers, on the other. These two factors directly affect the internal rate of return."

We look at each other triumphantly, but I'm quick to dampen the mood. "So, we tied all four goals to one primary goal. Hooray for us. But how does that help us run the DOT's projects?"

Raji pauses for a minute, and says, "We need to look at some examples. Randy said the goal function should allow everyone to compare between alternatives. If we understood him correctly, that means calculating the value of the function for every alternative and comparing them to see which contributes more value."

"Let's take an example," I say, "something that happened just recently. For road 612, we deliberated between putting up a reinforced soil wall or a regular concrete wall. The first would have cost two hundred and fifty thousand dollars more than the latter but would have cut the length of the project by a month. How do you calculate which is preferable?"

We both think about it for a couple of minutes, and eventually agree that you don't have to calculate all four aspects of the goal function, it's enough to compare just the two elements that are directly involved in this instance—cost and duration. At this point, we get stuck trying to translate time into monetary terms. We decide to put aside precise calculations and settle for an estimate. "We pay the contractor one hundred million dollars for building the road," I say. "We can assume that the cost of design, land expropriation, and compensation to the infrastructure companies for relocating their systems from the road's path would pretty much double the budget, meaning about two hundred million dollars. Let's assume the government wouldn't have approved the road's construction without an internal rate of return of at least twelve percent per year. Twelve percent a year is about one percent per month, and one percent of two hundred million is two million—"

"That means," Raji jumps in, "that if you'd put up the reinforced soil wall, then, on the one hand, the taxpayer would pay two hundred and fifty thousand dollars. But on the other hand, the same taxpayer would earn two million dollars by starting to use the road a month earlier. Eight times as much." He looks at me and shakes his head, "That's a pretty good deal."

"That's right," I say, a chill of excitement and pride run through my body, "that's a pretty good deal. And also, I think we just cracked Randy White's formula. The project's goal function is its IRR, the internal rate of return. Every action that increases it is good. Every action that decreases it is bad. The total monetary value of changing costs and changing duration tells us if the IRR has increased or decreased, and therefore—whether the action is worthwhile or not."

## 21. THE ROAD CAN BE HASTENED

"How long are we gonna wait here?" Josh asks as I kill the engine where the paved road stops and the dirt service road begins. "Not too long. Vehicles pass here every couple of minutes."

"And are you sure they'll stop for us and takes us to that camp you said?"

"Of course. Don't forget, I still know everyone around here."

It's true. Just one month ago, I was still running this whole operation. And even though I haven't been to visit here since I started working for the DOT, to avoid any claim about conflicts of interest, were I to simply walk into the project manager's office, it wouldn't take me more than a minute to take control over the entire project again.

"But they know we're coming, right Dad?"

"Not exactly." Josh looks at me with suspicion, and I explain that we haven't set a formal meeting. Still, I'm prevented from working on the 612, which is why I'm here at 5:15 p.m., in my private car, with my youngest son tagging along. *Business meeting? What are you talking about? Just a day out with my little kid…*

Chambers had promised I wouldn't need to work with Ethan and Danielle, but I forgot that even he answers to someone no less assertive than him, the governor of the state, in an election year. The 612 is supposed to be inaugurated prior to the elections, and the governor is doing everything in his power to explain to Chambers why that better happen. The amount of driving time this road will save is valued at about two million dollars per month, by no means an insignificant sum—but even more than money saved, the governor is worried about enquiries that will uncover inefficiencies and "a waste of taxpayers' money"—a politician's worst nightmare.

Following a conversation behind closed doors between Chambers and the governor, it was decided to send me over to speak informally to Ethan, no protocols or binding promises, just to see what else could be done so that the governor's election campaign will include a photo op of the new road's inauguration.

I've seen Ethan a couple of time since I "defected" to the DOT, but we still haven't really discussed work matters—at least, not in the sense of two people on opposite sides of the same project. Ethan gave an emotional speech during my farewell party; a week after, I was invited to one of the company accountants' sixtieth birthday party; last week, when Ethan came to the DOT building to speak with Chambers, he stopped by my office for a coffee before heading back to the site.

Now, however, even in an unofficial capacity, I'm going to need to talk business.

"Dad, how long is this gonna take? I'm bored!" Right before I'm about to lose my patience with Josh, a truck pulls up with tires screeching next to us. "How you doin', boss?" As the cloud of dust settles, I see Kevin's face smiling at us. "Hop in."

During the short drive in, I get the impression that there were no major breakthroughs since I left the site. True, looks can be deceiving, even for an experienced engineer—progression on a project such as this is not always linear, and of course part of the work is done underground—but still, according to the plan, the road should be much more advanced than it is now.

"So, what brings you here, Eric?"

"I'm here to see Ethan, I thought we'd have a little chat. He should be here now, right?"

"Sure, the usual Tuesday 5:30 p.m. meeting. Don't tell me you'll be joining us?"

"Oh, no, no. I'm done switching sides," I feel slightly embarrassed as I answer. "What's going on with you guys? Making progress?"

"You know, same old story," he lets out a big sigh, suggesting that they are still dealing with setbacks. "We can work more or less without interruptions now, but we're having some trouble with the subcontractors because of all the delays. I don't need to tell you; they didn't exactly sit around and wait for us."

"They started other projects?"

"Of course. Luckily for us, none of them committed to any really big projects, but we're still occasionally short-staffed. But hell, I'm not here to complain."

The door swings open and Ethan welcomes me with a firm handshake which, to both of our surprise, turns into a sentimental hug. "Good to see you, even if you're on the villains' side!"

"What do you say, kid," Ethan turns to Josh, "what do you make of your daddy's new clothes?" he says and points to my tailored trousers and button-down shirt. "He's turned into a clerk, hasn't he?"

Josh smiles awkwardly, not sure what to say. "Don't be shy, Josh," I put my arm around his shoulder, "tell Ethan that the new job allows me to come home before sunset, and that the phone never rings on weekends."

"Right," my son says, and drops his gaze to the floor. Ethan offers me a coffee, but I refuse politely, saying that I don't intend to stay long.

"So, how can I help you, my friend?" Ethan asks. Looks like he understands I'm here on duty.

"That's exactly what I'm here to find out. We want to know if there's any way to shorten the schedule and finish the project earlier."

"I see," Ethan looks at me and Kevin, and then at Josh.

"I'm just checking, hypothetically," I take a step back, "no one's demanding anything here. We're not looking to bulk up Randy White's claims portfolio."

"Okay. I don't need to tell you that to cut a project such as this short is technically simple but requires a lot of logistics." That sounds like the start of a solution.

"Of course," I immediately reply, "let's hear it."

"Do you remember the road by Brown Peak, the one we had to finish by November before the snow set in?"

"Actually, I don't."

"Never mind. The point is, because time was of the essence, we filled the road in two shifts. The first layer by day, and the second layer by night. That enabled us to cut two months of construction down to one. In this case, we can cut down even more. Something like a month and a half, I would say."

He doesn't need to tell me the catch—paying for all the extra hours it would take to do such a job.

"And another thing," he goes on, "if you're really pressed on time, we could get a lot more heavy machinery in here, literally double the amount, to make headway on the earth-works down the road. Even without doing the math, I think it's fair to estimate that both of these things together can cut down the project's schedule by something like three and a half months."

"So, a one hundred percent increase in throughput of manpower and machinery."

"Not one hundred percent. I suppose more like seventy to eighty percent, no more. At night, the throughput is always smaller, and managing so much heavy machinery in a relatively tight space is no simple matter. You can't reach maximum output."

"I see," I say as Ethan's employees start coming in for their meeting. He points at his watch to say we should wrap it up.

"How much do you think it'll cost?" I remember the numbers from the plan to a certain extent but couldn't calculate the figures in my head while we were talking.

"You know I don't just throw numbers up in the air, right?"

That's true, Ethan has always been calculated and responsible enough to tell people to wait until the numbers could be processed accurately. "Yeah, I know, Ethan. But still, if you had to give an estimate?

"This is off the record, right? We're not negotiating here."

"Of course not!" I point at Josh, "I swear on my kid."

"Okay. So, I'd say something in the vicinity of two million." He probably notices the almost imperceptible change in my expression, and adds, "Maybe three million."

"I see," I say calmly, hoping that's good enough. On paper, paying three million dollars to save seven million dollars is a great deal. But in the real world, your expenses will be written on the balance sheet, but the public funds you saved by opening the road earlier won't be written anywhere.

"Okay, Eric, I gotta go to the meeting, I don't want to keep them waiting for me. So, Kevin will take you back to the road. We'll be hearing from you soon?"

"Sure."

He turns to Josh and gives him a playful punch on the shoulder, "You take care of your dad, kid. Alright?"

I can't restrain myself. I call Chambers immediately to tell him about the conversation with Ethan. He doesn't need convincing that two million dollars, or even double that, is worth investing to cut down the project's schedule. The governor would probably be very pleased to be presented with the new schedule, as well.

"Before you go ahead with the plans, though, we need to run it by our two friends," he reins in my excitement. "I'm guessing Greg's not going to be a problem because the plan is profitable, but you never know with Naomi."

"Why would a legal adviser object to such a clearly advantageous move?"

"I have no idea. She'll find something. We've made odder decisions in this office before, believe me."

## 22. MEETING THE DEMANDS OF THE LAW

When I first told my friends at Rhombus that I was taking a job with the DOT, their immediate reaction was contempt and scorn toward my new employers. I kept hearing things like, "you know it takes them two years there to move a pen from department to another," or "you're downgrading from 100 mph to 20 mph." But that's not the impression I got from Chambers—I felt that Chambers doesn't just come into work, he comes to work.

In the short time I've been here, that impression has been completely justified. The following morning after my conversation with Ethan at the site of the 612, I got a call from Chambers' secretary. "Mr. Price, Mr. Chambers requests that you come to the conference room at ten thirty," she said without waiting for an answer.

As I walk down the narrow corridor leading to the conference room, through the open door of the room I can see Chambers and Greg Nader chatting. As soon as I enter and close the door behind me, it swings right back open and Naomi walks in.

"Everyone's here," Chambers announces, "let's resolve this matter."

I like these kinds of meetings. No assistants, no protocols, no empty words uttered simply for the sake of providing an alibi later. No endless discussions over each minute legal and financial clause. In this kind of forum, you can speak freely, have a real discussion, and eventually arrive at an actual decision.

Chambers starts off with a brief presentation on where we are with the 612, including the delays incurred through a succession of mishaps—most notably, of course, the support wall—and casually mentions that the governor would be very pleased to see the project come to a prompt conclusion.

"Hold on, boss. You know that if the motivation here is the governor's own political campaign, we could be in trouble," Naomi interjects quickly with the legal perspective.

"I know, but this is not about politics. Not only, at least. Greg, could you explain?"

Sometimes I think the CFO goes to sleep at night hugging his little laptop. He smiles, buries his face in the silver screen, and explains the financial ramifications of delaying the project's finish date. After he sums up the expenses, he shuts the screen and looks directly at Naomi, "Therefore, for every month we finish the 612 earlier, we save the taxpayer something like one million nine hundred and seventy-eight thousand dollars." It's clear to see Chambers prepped him for this meeting.

"Thank you, Greg," Chambers turns to face me. "I don't think you two know, but yesterday, I sent Eric out on a mission behind enemy lines." He waits for some kind of surprised reaction from Greg and Naomi; when it does not arrive, he goes on, "Tell them about your accidental meeting with Ethan, please."

I feel bad to downplay the drama he has built up in his introduction, but I deliver a pretty dry account of the conversation I had with my previous boss, and the possible solution we arrived at.

"As you can see," Chambers quickly jumps in, "you don't need Greg's computer to see this is financially advantageous. We haven't crunched the numbers and gotten down to details with Ethan and the other contractors yet, but we're estimating we can save something in the range of four million dollars."

When Chambers finishes his sentence, a tense silence pervades the room and we all look around the table. Naomi crosses her arms on her chest and starts talking, "Yes, you know it's my turn now, and you're asking yourself, *how is she going to spoil the party this time*, right?" Actually, that's exactly what I'm thinking, and by the looks on their faces, so are Chambers and Greg. "Let me spare you the suspense. There's a legal issue here."

Chambers sighs loudly and mumbles under his breath, *I can't believe this crap.* Greg and I look at Naomi with disbelief, as she goes on. "It makes perfect sense that we call Ethan tomorrow morning—why, today, even—and agree on amendments to the contract, increased pay in return for expediting work and finishing early. But it doesn't work that way."

"How does it work, then?" I barge in, raising my hand slightly in apology.

"We work in a world of contracts, and that world has formal rules. When we signed a contract with Rhombus— and, if I remember correctly, you were there—" she looks straight at me, "that was after Rhombus won a tender with clearly defined terms. There is no clause in the contract regarding accelerating work for extra pay, and if there had been, someone else might have won the tender."

"So? That was two years ago. What's the problem now?" Greg asks.

"Isn't it clear?" Naomi looks at us impatiently, "It makes us felons."

"Felons?!" Chambers loses his cool. "That's a bit over the top, don't you think?"

"Absolutely not. We would be in breach of the law of tendering, and that's a felony. We can't afford that. Imagine one of the contractors who competed with Rhombus for the tender finds out about this and decides to sue us. For example, he might claim that he has surplus production capacity, meaning accelerating work doesn't cost him a thing. On the contrary, it allows him to utilize the full capacity of his equipment and manpower. In such a case, he could claim that had he known we would require paid work acceleration, he wouldn't have raised the price of his offer and thus he would have won the tender, instead of Rhombus. If the court would decide in his favor, it would file the case as damages for loss of profits, meaning, it could rule that we have to compensate the contractor for all the profits he lost by not winning the tender. The contractor would claim that the common profit margin in the field is five percent, so, on a hundred-million-dollar project, he would have stood to make five million dollars—which we, in our malicious evil-doing, robbed him of. You see, in such a case, we might find ourselves paying five million dollars to save four. Not exactly the deal of the century. And that's without even taking into account the bad press that will follow. How would we explain it? There are no lives at stake here that would justify paying extra for work."

I take a deep breath, and try to remind myself this nice

woman, whose command of the letter of law never ceases to impress me, is just doing her job. "Naomi, you mean to tell me that because of a contract we signed two years ago on a project that has since changed in almost every aspect and detail, we can't do what is clearly the right thing for us, the project, and the public?"

"If you choose to look at it like that," she answers calmly.

"Is there another way to look at it?" I can barely contain my anger.

"Of course. You're thinking only about this project, but I'm thinking about all of our projects. We run them in accordance with the law of tendering, the law that stipulates that no public body can purchase anything without a tender. As you know, the purpose of this law is to prevent corruption and maximize returns on investment of public funds. To do that, the law stipulates that we need to define our projects clearly and precisely and allow each contender to submit his price for executing the project. Once we change the conditions of the tender after someone has already won it, we are in breach of that law. Imagine what would happen if all our contracts were constantly changing. I mean, every project has its delays, right?"

She has a point.

"But not every project has such a clear and desirable solution," Chambers jumps to my defense.

"I'm an attorney, not an engineer. Just like Greg doesn't decide on which stone cladding to use but finds the budgetary means to fund it, I stick to my own field, too. I'm truly sorry, Martin, but I can't endorse this move from a legal standpoint."

# PART 3 | THE MANAGER'S DILEMMA

## 23. ELI GOLDRATT OR JOHN NASH

The road to Sally's house is starting to feel more and more natural. I don't use GPS anymore or even look at the highway signs, I just cruise down the road with country music playing on the radio. *Get ready, I've got a surprise for you*, read the sparse text from Sally two hours ago. How does one get ready for a surprise? Well, that's supposed to be my specialty—my entire career has been built on surprises, and not the good kind. But Sally's message doesn't refer to engineering setbacks or faulty design, and I decide to come prepared, if she's planning a grand romantic gesture, I'm going to dress accordingly. I trade in my regular jeans for a nice pair of black trousers, and my sneakers for my finest Italian leather shoes. I don't take any risks with my shirt and stop at the mall on my way over to get a new one. "You look great," the saleswoman tells me, and manages to sell me a sixty-dollar leather belt at the counter. She's good.

About sixteen miles away from Sally's house, my phone rings.

"Hey Eric, could you drop by the BP gas station at the 755 interchange?"

"Yeah, sure. What do you need?"

"There's a health food store there, and I need spelt flour and coconut oil. Don't forget, okay? It's really important."

I assure her I wouldn't forget, and a fifteen-minute drive

later, I pull up at the gas station. I see a Burger King, a Taco Bell, a small diner, and a convenience store—but that's it. No health food store, as far as I can see. But before I can pull out my phone to call Sally, I see her walking toward me with a grin on her face.

"I see you're gullible enough to believe that there would actually be a health food store at a place like this." I try to hide my embarrassment, but she storms me with a kiss. "Come on! We're going for a walk."

When we pull away from our hug, Sally suddenly notices my clothes. "Um, what are you wearing?"

I feel embarrassed again. I argue in my defense that she should have expected me to dress up when she told me to prepare for a surprise. "No big deal. Do you still have a pair of sneakers in your car?" I do. As I change my footwear, Sally opens the car door and tosses a big duffle-bag to the back seat. She sits behind the wheel and says, "Are you ready?"

"With you? Always."

A hundred and fifty yards away from the station, a dirt path splits off the main road; Sally turns into the path with the confidence of a person who knows where she's going. "I hope you have car insurance," she remarks, and jabs me with her elbow when she sees I'm not laughing. "Don't worry, I know what I'm doing."

Within three minutes, we're on a path which starts between two large cornfields and continues into what looks like wild woodland. She stops the car when the road comes to a sudden and abrupt end, and we start walking through the woods. "Quiet," she quickly brushes away any attempt on my part to ask questions, "we're nearly there."

My clothes snag on thorns and are soiled by the tall damp grass, but after five minutes of walking through the woods, we reach a clearing.

"Well? What do you say?"

What can anyone say about a forest clearing? But I can sense I'd better tread lightly. "It's lovely," I say. "I know, isn't it?" She puts her bag down, pulls out a large blanket and spreads it on the ground. I'm still trying to figure out what's going on, and she's already placing rocks on each corner of the blanket. She pulls out a bottle of wine, two glasses, and some snacks. I take off my shoes and lie down on the blanket. Before I can complain about rocky ground poking into my back, Sally lies on me and covers my face with her wonderful head of curls. No complaints here.

We lie on our sides and look at each other while I stroke her flushed face. It's pretty clear what's going on—every date reinforces the feeling; every conversation makes the picture clearer. But the memory of the last couple of years of my relationship with Karen still hurts.

"I have two things to tell you," Sally says with a serious tone. "First of all, I bought the wine we're about to drink six years ago in northern Spain, and I've been waiting for the right occasion to drink it since."

"And this is the right occasion?" I ask, trying feverishly to recall if I'm missing some sort of important date here, like an anniversary or a birthday, or something.

"You and me, alone in nature. Could there be a better occasion?"

She's right. I sit up and uncork the bottle—a superb Rioja which, poured into two glasses, looks splendid. We clink our glasses, and the wine lives up to my expectation. I don't even need to feign excitement, and Sally can tell. "And what's the other thing?"

"Oh," she blushes, "I love you."

Before I can even process what she just said, my mouth beats my head to the punch, "I love you too."

\*\*\*

It's hard to believe, but despite the rocks and pine needles sticking poking into our backs, we manage to take a nap on the picnic blanket, exhausted and in love. When I wake up, with Sally's arms still wrapped around my body, I can see the sky starting to darken. I gently nudge Sally awake, we quickly wrap up our stuff, and head back to the car. I have no idea what this weekend will lead to, but what is certain is that I'll remember these moments in the forest clearing for a long time. In fact, I'll probably remember them for the rest of my life. At the gas station, she asks we sit for a while in the shabby diner, because she's still a bit tipsy from the wine and everything else.

We walk in, and before the waitress comes up to take our order, I remember that I sat here just recently. "Steer clear of their coffee," I whisper to Sally, "trust me. And if you think they have herbal tea—you're probably in for a disappointment."

I order two cups of Earl Grey, which seems like the safest non-alcoholic choice on the menu. Sally asks me where I know the place from. I tell her about my meeting with Nick Waters, the rugged wall contractor who gave me a free life lesson in project management. "So, you came to me after that conversation?" she arranges the chronology of events in her head.

"Sort of," I answer, and tell her all about the series of frustrating meetings I had during those stressful few weeks, the meeting with the designers, my official meeting with Danielle, my meeting with Randy White, and even our own first meeting at Tom's Café, when we bargained over the new wall's covering.

Sally remained silent for a minute, and then said, "You know, these stories really remind me of the prisoner's dilemma. Everyone has a separate contract whose rules make them act according to their own interests, which are completely different to the interests of the project. So, the project can't possibly be run efficiently. As a result, everyone is working in an environment which can't be made more efficient, and, consequently, their remuneration can't improve, either. This is a prime example of a case in which the system operational rules necessarily lead to suboptimal results. Just like the prisoners that are going to serve a five-year prison sentence instead of one, because the rules of the prisoner's dilemma don't allow them to communicate and build trust."

Wow. A few sips of hot tea, and she's sharp and focused again.

"Exactly," I get excited, "the analogy isn't exactly perfect, since in this case there aren't just two prisoners but a host of different actors with interests that clash at times and overlap at others. But the general picture is quite similar."

"And no one has any idea how to resolve it, right?" she insists.

"There was one person who almost cracked it, but his

solution was problematic." I tell her about Goldratt and the critical chain, how it can be applied efficiently to some projects, but not to others.

By this point, I'm not surprised to learn that not only does Sally know about Eli Goldratt, but she's read his books, as well. "If you are familiar with this theory, maybe you have some insights on how to apply it to our projects?"

"Eric, I intended for us to do something more fun than talk about work at a gas station," she signals that her patience has its limits. "But, if I had to dig deep into the subject, I'd look at the prisoner's dilemma, not at Goldratt."

"Why's that?"

"From what I know about Goldratt, his solution concerns transitioning from *local optimization* of production departments *within* a factory *to global optimization of the factory* itself, right?"

I nod, and suddenly, I see where she's going with this. "But for us, the problem is *resolving the conflicts of interest between bodies external to us*. That's a completely different issue. That's why Randy White said Goldratt's solution won't work for us." As I say these words, I am struck by the gravity of their significance; we're trying to take out a screw with a hammer, instead of getting a screwdriver. We're trying to use an old tool to solve a new problem.

"Exactly. Your projects require a solution for a problem of inherent conflicts of interest between a large number of different actors. That looks like a completely different game, much more pertinent to John Nash than to Eli Goldratt."

"John Nash? Game theory? Is that why you mentioned the prisoner's dilemma?"

Sally smiles without saying a word. Even though I feel a bit like a child whose smart teacher led him toward the right answer, I take the compliment.

"Dr. Erikson," I say as I take out my wallet and throw a couple of bills on the mucky table, "let's leave theory at that, and go back to your practical plans."

## 24. THE CLIENT'S CLIENT

This morning started bad and has since become increasingly worse. After a practically sleepless night, I drive toward the office with Sally still on my mind, when Chambers calls. I answer and say that I'll be in in a couple of minutes. "In where?" he practically yells his reply, "You remember we have a meeting with the governor in fifteen minutes, right?"

I've never driven this recklessly in my life. I'm overtaking cars like a drunk driver, committing traffic violations worthy of getting my license revoked for a long, long time. Eventually, I arrive just ten minutes late. Panting and embarrassed, I arrive at the governor's office, only to discover Chambers sitting by the reception desk holding a paper coffee cup. "We're going to have to wait a bit," he tells me dryly, as if I didn't just risk my and several other drivers' lives just to get here on time. He looks nervous, and, as he told me yesterday, "when the governor calls you in for a meeting that hasn't been planned two months in advance, it means one of two things, either he's in trouble, or you're in trouble. Usually, they're one and the same.

"Wait, is your computer here?" I probe, because I suddenly realize I don't have any documents or presentations we might need. He points with his eyes to his black briefcase. I sigh in relief. We go over our arguments again, about the vigorous work being carried out on the site and the creative solutions we have found to hasten the road's completion as much as possible. "It's best I do the talking, okay?" he turns to me, and I nod in agreement. Of course it's best.

At the governor's request, to the extent it can even be called a *request*, we arrive just the two of us, no legal advisers, no finance people, no assistants. "That means nothing's going to go on the official record, today," Chambers explains, "but in my experience, these are the most important meetings. We're going to have to deliver some answers." So we're here, with answers and reasons and explanations, and the governor's aging secretary approaches us with a smile like a flight attendant before landing. "Governor Graham will see you now."

The office of Governor George Graham is a bit illusive, at first. Its proportions resemble a basketball court, long and narrow. You have to turn your head to see his giant desk. "Gentlemen, come in," I hear his voice before I see him. It takes my mind a second to reconcile the famous figure from the news on television with the person standing before me now. We step on the thick carpet adorned by the state emblem and approach the heavy hardwood furniture. A couple of flags on both sides of the table indicate that this is no regular office, and the eyes of past governors peering at you from oil paintings mounted along the wall closely examine you and your business here. A tall stack of papers is neatly placed on the desk, almost blocking the governor's chair from our sight.

"If it isn't Mr. Chambers," the governor opens. "You must be asking yourself why I am inviting you here now, in the middle of such a busy time, when the election campaign has already begun, and we have several difficult changes to make in the state budget."

Actually, we know quite well why we're here.

"Governor Graham," Chambers adds a little celebratory pomp to his voice, "your office hasn't informed us what's on today's agenda, but we have a couple of guesses."

"Okay, Martin, let's talk business." The governor puts an end to the formalities, "It's about the 612. I need it done." There seems to be little to no patience in his voice.

"That's what I thought. We have a pretty clear schedule," Chambers says and presents his briefcase to Graham, "we'd love to show you how we're moving along with the new plan."

"No need, Martin. I don't have time for any more graphs and presentations. You see this?" he points to the stack of papers, "These are the urgent matters I absolutely have to take care of this month. I don't have time for any more papers." Chambers and I exchange glances. We get the hint— we're a nuisance.

"Mr. Governor, we can give a little nudge, perhaps convince a couple of contractors to pick up their pace. When did you want the road done by?"

"Yesterday," Graham answers without a hint of humor. "You may not know this, but our neighbors across the border are going to renovate Highway 51 in six months. You know what that means, don't you?"

He sees the look of surprise on our faces. "Yes, I just learned about it too. Imagine the Highway 51 closed and the 612 not yet in operation. The gridlock will be on national news."

He doesn't have to explain it to us. Sometimes in life, events occur that make you want to tear out your hair in frustration. "Can't they wait just a little bit?" Chambers asks, not expecting the governor to answer him. Graham just looks at him and runs his hands through his silver hair. "They're saying that this was the original plan, and that we're the ones who didn't update them on the delays to the 612, so they didn't push back the Highway 51. They're saying that there's nothing they can do now. The contracts are signed, the ink is dry."

"Martin, there aren't going to be any more meetings," the governor goes on in a solemn tone. "I'll say this just once, in this forum only: you have to finish the 612 in five and a half months. If you don't, I might be out of a job by spring. And if that's the case, you might be out of a job, as well." Even without knowing my way around the internal politics, I can see by Chambers' reaction that the governor doesn't issue these kinds of threats on a regular basis.

"Mr. Governor," I feel the need to intervene when I see Chambers hasn't got anything else to say, "we're talking about cutting the work time in half. You're not asking us to hurry up, you're asking us to do magic."

Graham eyeballs me. "You're Price, right?"

I nod.

"Listen, Price. I'm surrounded by people who are experts at telling me why things can't be done. Those who rise up the ranks here are those of the other stock, the kind that get back to me, tell me that they're done, and ask what else they can do. This isn't the first time your road has made it into my office under such circumstances, and frankly, I've had just about enough of it. I know that according to the original plan, it should be finished five and a half months from now. I was patient when you told me about unforeseen delays, but now I need you to show me that just like it's possible to extend a project's execution time, it's possible to expedite it, as well. Five and a half months. As far as I'm concerned, you can be in touch with my chief engineer on a daily basis, you can ask any county in the state for assistance, and any request to move machinery will be approved automatically."

"Mr. Governor," I say, "such an increase in intensity will cost quite a lot of money—"

"Mr. Engineer," he replies before I can finish, "not increasing the intensity will cost quite a lot of money, as well. Three hours in a traffic jam, times thirty thousand cars, times two hundred days, times twenty dollars for every hour lost— that's quite a lot of money, wouldn't you say? And that's not even taking into account the non-financial implications."

Chambers jumps in before I can answer, "We understand, Mr. Governor. Eric and I will do everything in our power and beyond to get this done."

"That's what I wanted to hear," Graham says, and the first hint of a smile appears on his face. "Now, excuse me. I have two kindergartens to visit before lunch."

## 25. EVERYONE HAS A GOAL FUNCTION

By now, when Randy White enters the DOT building, he walks in like a superstar—all eyes are on him, and not because of the flashy gold bracelet he added to his look today. The employees here have been so impressed by the eccentric maverick and his creative mind that he's become the main topic of conversation this week. This time, we're back in the conference room. Randy settles in naturally at the head of the long oval table. Before he starts talking, Chambers stands up and addresses everyone, "Friends, before we begin, I want to bring you up to speed about something that happened this morning." He goes on to describe in detail our meeting with the governor two hours ago. When he's done, he turns to Randy and says, "What I just said means that we can't settle for a theoretical lesson with homework this time. If there's anything you know that can help up perform the impossible task that we've been assigned this morning, now's the time to tell us. In the situation we're in, we'll consider anything outside the box, even outlandish and crazy ideas. What we can't consider are impractical ideas that can't be executed in real life."

Randy White stands in the narrow space between his seat and the wall, and thanks Chambers. "One thing, though, Martin," he says, as if fleetingly, "we're definitely going to present solutions today, but they are not detached from theory. I promise, everyone will leave here with a clear idea about what to do and how to do it, but it won't work without understanding the theoretical part, first."

"*We* are going to present?" Chambers asks a little too loudly.

"What did you think?" Randy winks at me, "That I was going to do your work for you? Price! The stage is yours."

Last night, when we spoke over the phone, I was still uncertain. I briefly explained to Randy what Raji and I managed to arrive at. He listened in silence, and just when I thought the call had been disconnected, he said, "Excellent. I need you to explain this tomorrow at the meeting. Goodbye," and he hung up without allowing me to respond.

I remain in my seat, but all eyes are on me—including Chambers, who is taken by complete surprise.

Giving a speech after Randy White would be a challenge for anybody, but he leaves me no choice. "I don't know if everyone here knows him, but there's a young man here who until a couple of days ago I knew nothing about, except for his name. Raji, stand up please." Raji stands up, embarrassed by the attention, and I stand up as well. "Raji and I dedicated a lot of thought, together and apart, to crack Mr. White's assignment from last week—to define our goal—and eventually, we succeeded. I'm pretty sure I would not have succeeded without his help, so, first of all, thank you, Raji."

After a polite round of applause, I start presenting our thought process. I explain the new perspective we need to take when examining our projects, and boil it down to one sentence: "The project's internal rate of return is equal to the value it delivers to its users, divided by the cost of its construction and maintenance."

"When the value is greater than one," I explain, "it's good.

When it's lower than one, it's bad. Our goal is simple—increase that value as much as possible. Therefore, any time we have more than one way of executing something, we need to choose between our alternatives according to a simple criterion—which of the two ways would bring higher value to the project. As you know, the return on investment for roads is somewhere in the vicinity of twelve percent a year, approximately one percent per month. That was also the case with the 612, until our little chat with the governor this morning. One percent per month means that if we finish the project—which costs two hundred million dollars—one month ahead of schedule, we save two million dollars. That number was our way of comparing alternatives. If we find an arrangement in which we can finish a month earlier, and that arrangement costs us less than two million dollars, then that's the right decision to make. If the cost exceeds two million dollars for that month, it's the wrong decision. However, since this morning, that number has changed. Can anyone guess to what number?"

To my surprise, the person who answers immediately is Jill Sommers, the DOT's information systems manager. "Thirty-six?" she asks in a high-pitched voice. "Thirty-six what?" I pretend I don't understand, and she immediately replies, "Thirty-six million dollars a month. That's the value of three hours in a traffic, times thirty thousand cars per day, times twenty days a month, times twenty dollars per every lost hour."

Every head in the room turns to look at her. Half the people in the audience are engineers, and there's one or two among them that could make such a calculation in their heads—the rest pull out their phones and do the math on their calculator app.

I wait for twenty seconds, and when everyone agrees the numbers add up, I shush them and continue. "This number is so astronomical, that it actually means that anything we do to hasten the project, whatever the cost, is worth it. In other words, we have the financial incentive to resort to any means necessary. When Mr. White spoke about the connection between theory and practice, he meant that when we define the goal function of the project like I just did, we can easily calculate the conversion rate between time and money, so we can rationally prioritize our alternatives."

"Thank you very much for that impressive presentation, Price. I don't know if the DOT gives out bonuses," he says and lingers for a moment, knowing perfectly well that there are no bonuses at the DOT, "but you and that young man over there deserve a nice reward for your work. You wouldn't believe the amount of money you'll save if you stick to these ideas."

Chambers smiles and holds himself back from answering.

"Let's sum up what we've learned," Randy continues. "Our goal is to build roads in an efficient manner and give the public the highest-value product we possibly can when the internal rate of return—the road's IRR—is our relevant index. Over the years, all sorts of methods were developed to reach that goal, and we've grown so accustomed to those methods, that we've lost track of the fact that they are only a means to an end—not an end in and of themselves. One of the methods we developed was putting the project up for tender, where contactors compete against each other for the job. Our goal was to bring down the price of execution by competitive tendering because a low execution price increases the project's IRR. For the sake of the same goal, we allow bidders to offer alternative ways to execute the project. The alternatives proposed by the contractors should lead to an increased IRR. They can do so by offering a reduced price, a shorter execution period, or by providing a superior product which would increase public safety or require less maintenance. At the end of the day, the tender is not a goal in itself, but merely a means to increase the value of the project and obtain a higher IRR for the public. Does everyone agree, so far?"

Even I find myself nodding along vigorously.

"So, if we're talking about the 612, we can already identify one major constraint—its legal framework." Randy focuses his gaze on Naomi, and smiles that smile I've come to know so well. "Ms. Griffin, as the senior legal adviser in this building, could help us sort out the matter?"

After twenty years of litigation, a person loses the capacity to stutter—but in these few minutes, Naomi comes as close to that as possible. She skips the importance of keeping the letter of the law and focuses on the broader ramifications of breaking the law of tendering, until Randy stops her. "When you say 'broader ramifications', you mean that other contractors in other projects, which do not face the same kind of emergency as the 612 does, would come to us and demand that we change the design of their projects, or pay them to expedite its execution?"

"Of course," she replies.

"If we agree to their demands, on the basis of the same

logic we are now applying to the 612, what could the damage be?" he asks.

"This office carries out two billion dollars' worth of projects a year. If we open this loophole in all of them, it could amount to crazy sums. In one single year, we could lose everything we save on the 612."

"I think I didn't make myself clear," Randy lowers his voice and takes a long look at Naomi. "I didn't mean that we pay other contractors on other projects the same sums as the 612, I only ask what will happen if we apply the same rules? If we make our decisions based on the goal of maximizing the projects' value. If for regular projects—in which the value of expediting the execution is worth only one percent per month—we pay contractors half a percent to finish a month earlier. Then what would happen?"

Someone from the other side of the room says, "It's a win-win situation."

"That's right," Randy says. "We get a result that is better for the drivers on the road and better for the contractor executing the project. The only thing we need in order to remove that legal obstacle is to announce in advance, when we draft the tender, that that's what we are intending to do."

Randy turns around, opens his bottle of water, pours out a cup, and sips it slowly, allowing everyone in the audience to process everything that was said over the past hour. Right before people start chatting among themselves, he turns again to Naomi and says, "Like yourself, I too have been to court many, many times in my life. What do you think a judge would say if you explained that you had to decide between two different legal demands—the first, defending the competition, as required by the rules of tendering, and the second, defending the contractor's right to propose alternatives, also required by the same rule? Had you chosen the first alternative, you would have done so at the expense of tens of millions of dollars a month of taxpayers' money, while the second alternative would have prevented that damage."

He doesn't wait for an answer, and continues, "Therefore, I think the 612 case is one you would win for certain. It's also the situation with all of your other projects; the basic situation is the same, only the conversion rate between time and money is different. If you want to play it safe, just put into your contracts a clause stipulating under what conditions you will consider and approve a paid expediting of work. I'm sure that if any contractor in the future will sue you for not approving him what you approved for the 612, you'll win that case, as well."

When Randy finishes, a silence falls over the room. Everyone seems to agree with what he just said, including Naomi Griffin. But these kinds of moments tend to be short lived.

"Excuse me, Mr. White?" Raji raises his hand.

"Well, our top student has a question. Please, go ahead."

"I can see how the project's goal function helps us make the legal decision, but is that enough? Say Ms. Griffin will give her backing to pay the contractor to expedite his work, and say Mr. Nader," he looks over at the CFO, "finds the budgetary means to pay for the work—is that enough to guarantee we will finish the project in five and a half months?" I think Raji just expressed what's on all of our minds right now.

"I see Eric was right about you," Randy says. "That's

precisely the right question to ask. The answer is, of course, no. Absolutely not." He lifts his gaze from Raji to look at everyone in attendance, "Do you have any idea as to why that's not enough? What could make us fail?"

"Sure," Greg Nader says, "contractors will promise everything for money, but they will not promise to keep their promises. So we end up paying double, and still finishing late." The murmurs around the room suggest Greg is not the only to have developed a distrust of contractors. "Usually, contractors have limited crews available," he continues, "so in order to work faster, they need to hire crews from other contractors, which significantly increases their costs. Since they don't want to increase their costs, they have every reason to make promises but no motivation to keep them."

"And besides," says Dan Fox, one of the younger guys in the projects department, "even if the contractors intend to keep their word, most of the job is carried out by subcontractors, and they didn't even promise."

Dorothy, the head of Dan's team, whose last name I forget, joins in, "I think the problem is even bigger with subcontractors. In order for them to profit, they need to operate their crews constantly, meaning that they need available assignments to employ their crews at all times—even if some unforeseeable delay disrupts their schedule. Consequently, they usually keep very few crews on-site, and arrange it so that they have several different places where they can apply them on-site, so that in case of a disruption in one place, they can quickly relocate the crew to another place in the project and operate it there. When we ask them to bring in a lot of crews and work simultaneously wherever they can, any disruption will mean they will have crews with nothing to do, and they will lose money. In other words, hastening the work is good for us, but it's bad for them."

Randy stops this torrent before it rages any further. "That's right. In fact, the meaning of what you all just said is that we're not the only ones with goal functions, but also the contractor and subcontractors. If we examine the situation a bit deeper, we'll see that the same is true for the designers and our project manager, as well as any other body that has any stakes in the project. We're talking about a multi-partic-ipant project, in which every participant has their own goal function—whether they call it that or not."

He pauses for a moment and looks around at everyone in attendance. He then reaches into his crocodile-skin briefcase on the table besides him. He takes out a thick booklet and raises it up with one hand for everyone to see its cover, then takes a look at it himself and reads out, "**Reinventing Con-struction: A Route to Higher Productivity**." He looks at the audience again and says, "This is the most up-to-date and encompassing report on the construction industry there is at the moment. It was written by the leading management con-sulting firm in the world, McKinsey Company, and it came out in 2017. It contains more than one hundred and sixty pages of invaluable data and analysis. But I would like to read you all just one excerpt from it. This is what McKinsey defines as the most important issue." He clears his throat theatrically, and reads with emphasis, "An environment of misaligned contractual and incentive structures…"

He pauses again to make sure everyone is following. "In order to execute projects, we need dozens of participants, each of which has a goal function ingrained within their contracts. This contractual environment creates the conflicts of interest McKinsey is talking about. In order for all of the project's participants to pull in the same direction, we need to restructure contracts so that everyone's goal function will align with the project's goal function. We need to create a situation in which whenever anyone takes an action to maximize their own goal function, they will in fact be advancing the project. If we fail to integrate everyone's goal functions, everyone will work toward their own interests at the expense of the project."

"That's exactly what happens to us all the time!" Chambers suddenly jumps in. "Everyone pulls in a different direction."

Randy nods in satisfaction, pleased to see his points are getting across.

"So, what's the solution?" Once again, Raji reflects the general mood in the room, that it's time Randy delivers us from the labyrinth he's been walking us through for the last hour.

To my delight, Randy answers, "The answer is simple— you need to pay everyone to maximize the project goal function."

"Excuse me, but isn't that what we're already doing?" Chambers asks.

"What you're doing now is paying the designer to make designs, not for those designs to maximize the value of the project. You're paying the contractor to finish the project at a time you dictate, but you don't pay him to cut that time short—and the result is that he doesn't try to cut it short. Further down the line, the contractor hires subcontractors whose interest is to maintain constant work for their crews. Like Dorothy explained, to maintain constant work, they need to have more assignments than crews available to execute them at any given moment. So, it's not in their interest to speed up by investing more resources which are going to consume all their open assignments. A schedule planned by the critical path method does not provide the subcontractors with constant work, and since in order to profit they have to maintain constant work—they do not follow that schedule. You just don't know about it, because the schedule is updated only once a month and reflects the month that passed, and they use that to hide what they actually worked on."

Randy pauses the flow of his speech and looks at me.

"When you choose to use the critical chain method, things get even worse. That method creates a plan that forces subcontractors to skip from one assignment to the other even more than the critical path method does. Since the critical chain method increases these work inconsistencies for the subcontractor, the chances that they will follow a plan based on that method are even smaller."

I look around me, and everyone is stunned. What Randy White is telling us is that the entire way we go about our business is fundamentally wrong. But he doesn't stop there.

"What you should have done is offer a tender based not on the lowest bid, but on the highest goal function value. In other words, the contractor who can provide the best combination of price and duration should win the project. But that's just the start. For the primary contractor to be able to keep the short execution time he proposes, his schedule must allow his subcontractors to work constantly and efficiently, and in cases where that's not possible—he should pay them for the stops and starts. Otherwise, they simply will not stick to the schedule…"

He pauses once again, to make sure everyone is listening.

"Furthermore, in order for the primary contractor to be able to finish on time, the designs he receives should be good enough to require very little changes during their execution, and when making changes to the designs is unavoidable, your designers should provide them quickly, so that they don't delay the contractor's work."

I can see heads nodding around me. Someone ever mutters that designers are the main problem.

"In order for that to happen, you need to direct the designers toward your goal function, as well," Randy continues as if he did not just change the topic. "Currently, you're paying them simply to provide designs. Just designs. What you need to do is to pay them to create designs that will not require changes as the work progresses…" he pauses to emphasize, "Part of the designers' wages should be paid for *changes that are not made*, because the fact that there are no changes being made is what allows the contractor to finish his work on time and maximize the project's value. And still, in places where changes are unavoidable, you should pay them to design the change as fast as possible so the contractor can continue without delay. If you don't do that, the designers will hinder the contractor's ability to maximize the project value…"

He pauses again, takes another sip of water, and concludes, "Last but not least are your project managers. They are the ones that need to make the tough calls. They're the ones that need to decide what to do when the contractor offers to cut the project short by one month for an additional million dollars. As things stand today, your entire conduct revolves around the question of how to keep the contractor from filing claims against you. To avoid claims, your project managers avoid giving the contractor any kind of instructions. The result is that your projects suffer from lack of decision-making and an absence of timely instructions. As long as all you take into consideration is the legal liability, then that can somehow be justified. But as soon as you take into consideration the value the project produces—and that value is influenced not just by a sum ruled by a judge, but by added costs and added time due to indecisiveness at the decision-making level—that can no longer be justified. Your people need to make decisions. They need to make them on the basis of the project's goal function, and they have to make them fast, despite the many uncertainties. You need to pay them to make those tough calls, and you need to withhold pay from them if they don't make them on time. As things are now, you are doing the opposite."

Listening to Randy White is hypnotizing, and the large conference room is dead silent as he continues, "If you want to improve, you need to orient yourselves toward maximizing your projects' value, not toward minimizing their cost. In order to do so, you need to orient your contractors' goal function, as well as that of your designers and project managers, to align with your own goal function."

As he lets the final sentence linger in the air, three slow claps are heard. It's Chambers.

"Very nice, Mr. White," he says. "Very nice, indeed. I'd love to speak with you at greater length when time permits. But I remind you where we started the conversation, we have to conclude with a plan of action. I'll accept everything you just said, if you can use it to help us finish the 612 in five and a half months."

"I was getting there," Randy answers directly, and turns back to the audience. "Going back to the 612. There are currently only twenty heavy machines working on-site in one shift, five days a week. I would start by doubling that amount to forty machines working two shifts per day—four times the current output. That means the contractor would have to rent expensive equipment he does not own, and work with reduced efficiency since he would have to crowd a lot of heavy equipment in small spaces. I propose you readily pick up the check for that inefficiency and throw in a nice bonus for the contractor's efforts. The sum of money that added expense will amount to will pale in comparison to the sum you'll be saving by preventing months of traffic."

He wraps up by saying, "That, of course, is just the general direction. On top of that, Mr. Price and I will go to the site and see what can be done about the critical path itself. It is most likely possible, and quite desirable, to give it special treatment."

# 26. A FAMILY PRISONER'S DILEMMA

Once again, I find myself in this rundown gas station, sat at a table in the same shoddy diner. This time, I am completely alone, sitting and staring at a bottle of beer that's been resting on my table for the past half an hour. I didn't expect to find myself in such a situation on Sunday afternoon, certainly not after the wonderful start to the weekend. But my life has taken so many sharp turns recently, that I'm practically used to it by now.

Two hours ago, we were still sitting in Sally's lovely garden (all organic, of course), joined by her two kids, Bianca and Aaron. I taught them how to play Whist; I even let Bianca win one round, to keep the mood jovial. They were born eighteen months apart, but Bianca, the eldest, who's just slightly older than my son Josh, is much more mature than her brother—just like my family. They were both pleasant and polite; it's clear Sally did a good job twice—both in raising them, and in preparing them for our meeting. When Aaron complained that they don't get to eat junk food with their mother, I promised him I'd take him to the restaurant of his choice. "Carl's Junior!" he shouted immediately. Sally was both delighted and disapproving at the same time.

After we finished playing, the kids went out to meet friends, and, lying on her new rocking chairs, Sally and I toasted the successful introduction with a glass of wine. Her house is located on a large lot adjacent to a narrow, freshwater stream. When you close your eyes (and shut off the kids' music), you feel the serenity of nature.

"I've made a lot of mistakes with Owen throughout my life," her gaze scans the length of the green landscape, like a drill sergeant during roll call, "but this house is one of the best decisions I ever made." I've gotten used to hearing that name, Owen, Bianca and Aaron's father, but I still can't keep the picture of them together out of my mind, happy and in love, like Karen and I were twenty years ago, or how Sally and I are now.

"I still haven't given you the full tour." She gets up from her chair. "Come on, I want you to get to know this place."

*The full tour* turns out to be much more serious than I had imagined; we dwell on each tree, stop by each bush to learn why it was planted in this particular spot. At the peak of the tour, we climb a tall ladder straight to the highest point of the roof. "Now you can really see my work," she says proudly as the wide range of botanic colors and textures are revealed in a panorama in front of us. It truly is impressive.

"I've been thinking about something for a while now," she says after we scale back down the ladder. I mumble something, but she goes on without waiting to hear what I'm saying. "I don't know, maybe it's too early... But, after today, we can talk a bit about the future, can't we?"

I tell her she's completely correct. I share her feeling that we've passed the dating stage, and that this relationship is worth examining deeper. What do I even mean by that? I'm not really certain.

"So," she takes a deep breath, "my old friend from college, Dianne, paid me a visit. She just so happens to be an excellent architect. I told you about her, right?"

"The one that opened an office with her divorcee?"

"Exactly. So, anyway, Dianne was here, and I naturally told her about you and the kids. You know how architects are addicted to drawings, right? So, I took out the house's blueprints, which I still keep a hard copy of, and we started playing around."

"Playing around?"

"You know, imagining all kinds of changes and additions. Ten minutes in, I turned on my laptop, and Dianne made a quick preliminary sketch. At first, we were just fooling around, but I was looking over it again this morning while you were sleeping, and I suddenly felt that it just might work."

Sally is very excited, but I'm still confused. "I'm sorry, honey, what sketch are you talking about?"

"Well, we'll have to go down to the living room. It's hard to explain it from here."

Some architecture software I'm unfamiliar with loads on Sally's computer, the kind intended for private residencies. As I soon find out, the software goes into the most minute details—from the color of faucets to sitting angles in the dining room. A black rectangle delineates Sally's house, and a red broken line adds space to its south and west wings. "You see, this way we can easily fit in two extra bedrooms, which, together with Owen's study, leaves enough space for everybody."

Only now does it dawn on me what she was talking about this whole time. "Is this your way of telling me you want us to move in together?"

"I think so. Anyway, you're dating an architect now… This is how we show affection."

I laugh.

"And also like this," she adds, pressing her lips against mine.

Suddenly, the front door opens. We manage to break away from each other just before we cause another awkward scene. It's Bianca, who's forgotten her earphones and has come in with her friend to get them while her friend's mother waits for them in the car. "Good thing we were just getting started," Sally says after Bianca and her friend leave, "it's too soon for her."

"But not for us," I say and point with my eyes toward the computer screen and Dianne's sketch, which looks quite professional—not exactly a playful and casual doodle.

"What are you saying?"

"Your friend is talented. I mean, not as much as you, but she knows what she's doing."

"I'm not talking about the sketches, Eric. What do you say to the idea, in general?"

"In general? It's always nice to renovate," I tease her.

"Be serious!"

"Alright, alright," I try to buy some time. "I expected this to come up sooner or later. Perhaps not this early, but don't worry. You're not going to scare me off with plans for the future."

"You don't know how relieved I am to hear that," she sighs and runs her hand through her hair, "I was starting to worry that I'm crazy."

"I don't see the contradiction," I keep teasing her, and she strikes me lightly on my cheek.

"Haven't you learned to be careful, by now? You know I

can be dangerous."

I look at the screen again, and I notice a mark in small letters at the bottom of the sketch—*Draft 3*, and yesterday's date. I realize now how serious Sally actually is. This is a sketch Dianne dedicated time to working on in her office.

Sally notices I'm examining the sketch, places her hand on my shoulder, and takes command of the mouse pad with her other hand. She points the cursor to the broken line, "You see? I thought this could be Ashley's room. There's more privacy here, and we could even make a door out to the garden. It's a bit smaller, but she's going to go off to college soon, anyway." She keeps moving the cursor along the sketch and sneaks a look at my face. "And here we could put Josh and Ben."

"Wow." That's the only thing I manage to say, as I realize my life is about to change drastically. Suddenly, I feel overwhelmed by the significance of this step, which ten minutes ago was nothing more than a non-committal statement of intent, and is now, all of a sudden, delineated by borders, rooms, and doors.

"Right? I think so, too!" Like me, Sally is looking at her own world, but at this moment, I feel the two are completely disconnected. "At first," she goes on, "I thought this house was too big for us, so I focused my attention on the outside. But suddenly I feel like this is exactly what it was intended for, you know? An old couple in love, and five kids. Even in this familial mess."

From this point on, I hear what she's saying, but I'm no longer listening. While she's talking, I'm wondering if at any point in this fantasy of hers, my opinion was even taken into consideration.

Thoughts are running through my head fast, and slight reservation turns into major concern. I imagine what it would be like to live somewhere else—here, to be specific—being torn from my home a second time, rocking the already precarious balance between Karen and myself that the kids have gotten used to. So far, our love has felt unchained and carefree, but in reality, there are many things for me to take into consideration, and I can't just ignore them. Not now, at least.

"Sally, stop, please," I surprise both of us with a sudden stern change of tone, sounding like a boss scolding his employee.

The smile evaporates off her face, and the tiny wrinkles at the sides of her mouth are made prominent by the surprised look on her face. "It's too early, isn't it? I knew it," she retreats.

"It's not about timing," I say. I can feel the argument bubbling under the surface.

"Then what is it about?"

"Don't you find it a little odd that you've decided on your own that we'd all move in here?"

"I didn't decide anything, Eric."

"Then what do you call this?" I move the cursor around the sketch, "this seems to me like a decision."

"I don't see what the big deal is. You said yourself that we're on the path to the next stage, I just wanted to be prepared for when that moment comes. That's all."

She's always ready. And if she's not ready, then she's getting ready. I'm almost mad at myself for not seeing this coming.

"And, are you prepared now?"

"I'm not so sure anymore," the pitch of her voice rises, "I'm feeling under attack, here."

"That's odd, because that's how I feel, as well."

"You? Eric, I honestly don't know what you're talking about."

I can feel we are slipping down a dangerous slope, but instead of hitting the brakes, something inside propels me to hit the gas. "If you're prepared, can I see the sketch for my house, then?"

Sally doesn't even answer. She just stares at me with an incredulous look. I can see she doesn't fully understand the question but understands where it's leading.

"No, really. Where's the sketch for my house? Isn't it one of the possible scenarios? Did it even cross your mind that perhaps we'd move into my house?"

Going by her body language, I doubt there's anywhere at the moment that Sally would like us to live together.

It's too late to stop now.

We start off in a civil manner, with me explaining to her that it's hard for me to imagine leaving my house, that I also have kids and that I am reluctant to rock their world again. She answers that she understands, but that Aaron is an extremely sensitive boy who underwent a traumatic experience during the divorce, and that his psychologist made her swear she would avoid any other changes. "He's so attached to this house."

I remind her that Josh went through a similar process, and that even though he didn't go to therapy, I'm sure he was traumatized by the divorce. And there's also Ben, who's integrated so well to his new school.

Sally stresses that she's poured her heart and soul into this house, especially the wonderful garden which was a "dump" before she started taking care of it.

Eventually, I explain that if I lived here, it would add forty minutes in each direction to my daily commute, and that even now, I get home to the kids late when they stay with me.

I propose we take some more time to think things over. She responds by saying that time won't change the situation we're in, and that we'd just circle back to the same point.

I blame her for being self-centered, caring about what works for her first, and only then turning to think about others. She yells at me for being obstinate; she says I'm so afraid to leave my comfort zone that I'm missing out on life, and she doesn't see how anyone could grow and evolve living with a person like that.

Like an idiot, I say nothing and go up to the bedroom. I grab my bag and storm out the door, not before I tell I can see how much she invests in her plants, and that I'm the last person who would want to stop her from growing.

So, here I am, at the diner. The waitress keeps her distance, occasionally sneaking a glance at me. I guess you don't have to be too perceptive to see I'm going through something.

## 27. THE CLIENT'S OWN CONSTRAINTS

It's been half an hour since I had my morning coffee, and I'm staring aimlessly at my computer when Chambers' secretary calls and asks if I can go see him now. When I walk into his room, I see Greg Nader, the CFO, is also there. The two of them ask me to join them at the table. Chambers starts.

"Following our last conversation with Randy White, Greg held an important meeting in the finance department, to see how the DOT's goal function should affect their department. They came to some very interesting conclusions. It's probably best that Greg introduces them himself. Greg?"

The CFO starts by clearing his throat and taking a sip of his tea. "What Randy said was that we're wrong in the way we pay those who work for us. Since we are the ones in charge of payments in this organization, you can imagine we took it a bit personally. We asked ourselves—can we change some of these payments to a performance-based structure? Especially, payment for time, like Randy proposed. I won't bore you with the details, but the bottom line is that, accounting-wise, it's nearly impossible."

"Why is that?" I ask. "What do the rules of accounting care what you pay for?"

"Accounting doesn't care, but it also doesn't know how to work in nonmonetary terms. When we receive a budget for a road from the government, that budget is defined in absolute terms. X amount of dollars. Precise down to the last cent. What accounting doesn't know how to do is to provide a budget of X dollars plus Y days. The very foundations of accounting, the method by which we receive budgets and use them to allocate them to our contractors and suppliers, it's all in dollars and cents. There's nothing there regarding days and hours."

"I still don't see what the problem is," I say. "You know how to use dollars to pay for asphalt and concrete, why can't you use dollars to pay for days and weeks? If a contractor is entitled to a bonus for finishing his work three months early, why can't you pay him for it? Pay in dollars. Just like you pay for the asphalt he paves the road with."

"You don't understand," Greg says, "the problem is not us. We don't care. The problem is the bodies in charge of our budgets. Our budgets come from two sources—the local government and the federal government. Those two offices are staffed by finance people who don't know much about roads but know a great deal about money. In order for them to provide us with a budget, we need to tell them in advance exactly how much money we will need in order to construct a certain road, and they need to approve that sum. I can't come to them and say that the road will cost one hundred million dollars—but if the contractor works really fast, then it will cost one hundred and twenty million dollars. They don't work that way."

"This is no minor issue," Chambers joins in, "you have to understand that even the people who approve government budgets are just government agents, and they have their own principal-agent problem. Even when the state has a vested interest in finishing infrastructure projects as soon as possible because the savings exceed the expenditure, the budgets department only sees the expenditure—not the savings. It's the public which saves money, and the public does not run the budgets department. In the case of 612, the governor is helping us because the political pressure to prevent traffic is a strong enough incentive to call the budgets department to action, but that won't be the case in other projects. If we don't get the Department of the Treasury's backing, we won't be able to restructure how we pay everybody, and if we keep the current structure in place, we won't be able to change anyone's motivation."

"Listen," I tell the two of them, "I don't know much about money and finances, but I find it hard to believe that the budget people can't see past the expenses. I mean, if you take only expenses into account, then by the end of the project you're necessarily worse off then you were—because you can see the money spent, but not the valuable asset you created. In reality, it's the opposite way around. We take money whose market interest rate is two percent and turn it into an asset with an average annual yield of twelve percent."

"You are absolutely right, Eric, but I'm afraid that budget-wise, it's even worse than that," Greg says. "When we calculate the viability of the road, we do so in terms of increasing the state's productivity. Since taxation for that increased productivity is on average something like thirty-five percent, the revenue from the road that reaches the Department of the Treasury is thirty-five percent of its total revenue. In other words, for the Department of the Treasury, the road will always run at a loss, even if it is very profitable for the state. Do you see what I'm saying? The Department of the Treasury is an agent of the state, and it has its own principal-agent problem."

"Look," I say in despair, without speaking to anyone in particular, "I give up. I find it hard to believe economists work that way in practice, but I genuinely don't know. I think the right thing to do is to start a dialogue with the bodies that fund us, and ask them how they need it to be presented so that the clear economic advantage of expediting the road's construction will be reflected in their books as well—and not place them in a prisoner's dilemma of their own. I suggest that you, Greg, direct that question to them. In the meantime, I'll try to look at other directions."

## 28. APPLYING THE GOAL FUNCTION

"Why do you always have to talk about work?" Ashley complains as she takes our order—an Americano for me and a latte for Danielle.

"Because your dad is ruining his life, and, as usual, I have to save him from himself." I know my sister is kidding, but, still, her words sting. She waits for Ashley to go deliver our order to the kitchen, and then leans in and whispers, "Don't throw this away, Eric. I've seen what you two have together." She shakes a reproving finger at me, "People spend a lot of time looking for a relationship like that. You can't give up on it this easily."

"I'm not giving up yet, Danielle," I defend myself, "I just have trouble seeing how it's going to work at the moment."

"It'll work if you two decide to make it work. You know I never butt in on your private affairs, right? Well, I think this time you need someone to give you a wake-up call. You two are fighting like children over houses that are twenty-five miles away from each other? People would leave their country for a love like that."

She's not just talking about me, of course. I hear desperation in between her words, the high hopes and disappointments of the dating world. I can't help but love and appreciate her honesty.

Every time Ashley comes close, we quickly change the subject; when she finally takes off her black apron and sits at our table with a short glass of granita, we realize we'll have to continue our conversation about Sally some other time.

"So, what's new at work, Dad?" she senses we've gone quiet and tries to stir the conversation back up.

"You know, honey. Not much. I'm stuck trying to reconcile Randy's prisoner's dilemma theories with the reality of our projects at the DOT. But besides that, everything's fine."

"What theories?" she sits up in her seat, like an animal in a state of increased alertness. "Anything I can help with?"

"Someone's grown in confidence…" Danielle interjects. "I love it!"

"Actually, I do have an idea I'd like to try out on your aunt. Do you have time to hear it?"

Ashley scans the empty café and nods. "Sure."

I explain to the both of them our newfound insights about the project's goal function.

"Okay, so it's pretty simple," Ashley brazenly asserts, "you just need to identify your own goal function and make sure everyone else works in accordance with it." Having received no answer from me or Danielle, she starts to lose her patience, "What? Why are you smiling like that?"

"It's not that simple," Danielle starts explaining, "the person managing these projects doesn't work alone. In fact, in the business world, hardly anyone works alone. These projects have so many different factors to them that even if you identify your goal function—which is very important—there's no guarantee everyone else will work in accordance with it. Is that correct, Eric?"

"Absolutely."

"But you can't be responsible for everyone's goal function, right? You and Danielle, for example, you don't share the same goals, if I remember your disagreement from a couple of months ago correctly."

"Once the owner of the project has contracts signed with everybody, there really isn't much he can do. But while he's drafting the contracts, he determines everybody's goal function, because he defines what it is that he wants to pay for. If he drafts his contracts better, he could align everybody's goal functions to his own goal function."

"So, why don't you do it?" she asks.

"Because, until today, we never defined the owner's goal function. Instead, we always said there are four simultaneous goals—price, time, quality, and scope. The finance guy was in charge of cost, the schedule manager was in charge of time, the quality control guy was in charge of quality, and scope... well, I'm not even sure who was in charge of that. Each one of them cared for their own responsibilities. Conducting the orchestra was the legal department, which is responsible for drafting contracts. It added another goal—winning in court when we have claims filed against us. For that purpose, the legal department drew up contracts which helped us defend against claims, but hindered the project's execution, and, subsequently, led to more and more claims being filed against us."

"So long as we believed that if everybody does his best to promote his own local goal it promotes the project's goal, we could never have drafted better contracts. In practice, our contracts looked like patchwork, each patch attempting to resolve a local issue, and none of them geared toward the project's goal function."

"Dad, do we really need the history lesson?" Ashley's

patience is running thin. "Today, now that you've defined the goal function, there's no excuse not to orient yourselves toward it."

She looks at me with the impudent look of a girl who is mature enough to challenge her father, until she notices Andy over at the bar signaling her to tend to a new customer who just sat down.

"The kid is right," Danielle says in a pensive voice, "you need to reorient everything. Contracts, methodology, information systems… Everything." She pauses for a moment, then looks me in the eye and says, "It's like a relationship. After you come to the realization you want to be with someone, you need to adjust everything else to make it work. Things like a house, location, arrangements, and schedules."

"Hey, sis, can we please drop the subject? I promise—I hear you. But I'm not in the right mindset to continue this conversation. On the other hand, though, if you have something wise to say about the goal function issue, I'm all ears."

"Why don't you pay performance-based bonuses? For example, pay designers extra for changes and delays they prevent? Meaning, if I designed a good plan to start with, I get a bonus without doing anything, simply because you won't have to make changes down the line."

"I thought of that," I explain to Danielle and see that Ashley's back, listening to the conversation, "but Chambers shot the idea down."

"Why? What did he say?" Ashley interjects.

"He said he's not going to pay twice—once for making the designs, and a second time for having planned correctly. As far as he's concerned, that's extortion. And I see his point."

"But doesn't he see what's going on in the moment? That every single one of his projects fail to meet their deadlines? Doesn't he realize that's costing him more?"

"He does, but he doesn't want to pay twice for the same job. He proposes we divide the payment we give designers into two components. A permanent component, like it is today, and a varying component, which would be performance-based. The problem is, even he doesn't believe any designer would be willing to take a deduction in pay in return for a performance-based payment. Even if the total sum would be larger."

"Do you want my advice as a designer or as your sister?"

"Whichever. Beggars can't be choosers."

"Then, listen. You're on the government's side now, but you probably still remember what your biggest fear was when you worked for Ethan, right?"

"Of course I do. Being out of work. We were always on the hunt for the next project, to guarantee continuous work."

"So, that's exactly where we are, too. And I assume that's where anyone who makes his living off projects is, as well. Resting in the knowledge that we have a steady stream of projects is infinitely more important to us than making a few extra bucks on a particular project."

"You mean, commitment to other projects is your preferred bonus?"

"That's right. As you know, project managers and designers are selected in one of two ways. Either by tendering, whereby whoever submits the lowest offer wins, or based on the owner's personal preference, without tendering. Why are certain managers and designers chosen over others?

Previous experience and a good rapport. Do you see the problem? Instead of professionalism, you've got politics. If you don't have a system in place to compare the performance of different designers, then those who invest in internal politics—like inviting DOT people to dinners at high-end restaurants—gain an advantage. As they rub shoulders, they tell them all about their heroics and success stories, leaving an impression which eventually leads to more projects, even if the quality of their work is in fact mediocre. Just think, how many perfectly good and able professionals are blocked out of DOT projects, simply because you guys continue commissioning work from your friends?"

"Well, when you say *your friends,* you are referring to your own office as well, you know that, right?"

"Yes. But it's different with us," Danielle tries to vindicate herself. "You know we do an excellent job."

Of course I know.

We brainstorm a bit, and just as we reach a dead-end, Ashley surprises us again. "Say, doesn't this remind you of what we talked about ahead of my presentation?"

I don't have any patience for Ashley's studies at the moment. With all due respect, I have more important matters to deal with. But Danielle picks up on what my daughter is talking about.

"Eric, listen for a second. She might be on to something."

"Okay, let's hear it," I say in a *what have I got to lose* voice.

"By the way you describe it, it sounds like the contractual situation you're in leads to bad rules for the game. After a contract is signed, each player's self-interest is to do as little as he possibly can, to keep his costs down. The result is that the project's goal function decreases; and as the pie gets smaller, the slices each one of the players can get becomes smaller as well, and everyone loses. It's exactly like the prisoner's dilemma."

*Wow*, I think to myself. If that's what she's learning in school, you won't hear me say a single bad word about Greenfield's education system.

"And what do you propose we do about it?" I ask in amazement.

"Do you remember that we learned that the answer to the prisoner's dilemma rests in the iterated prisoner's dilemma? Both your contractors and your designers are recurring actors, so maybe you can look at it like an iterated prisoner's dilemma and apply a similar solution."

Danielle gives me a *look what we've raised here* look, and says, "Sweetie, that's a really good idea. The question is, how do we apply a game theory solution to the DOT's contracts?"

"In the prisoner's dilemma, the goal function aims to get the shortest possible jail sentence in one given situation, while in the iterated prisoner's dilemma, the goal function aims to get the shortest possible jail sentence in all future cases, together." Ashley says. I see she's trying to translate her solution into my terms.

"And how do you link that to the DOT?" I ask her.

"I don't know enough about these things, but Danielle says that what she wants most are not bonuses for individual projects, but assurances that she'll be awarded more projects. So, maybe—"

"I think I've got something," Danielle interrupts. "Let's assume that instead of evaluating us on the basis of rapport and gourmet meals, you give every designer and contractor that works with you a grade for their performance on the project, and a good grade will be part of the criteria when you select someone for the next project. That will tie our goal function to the project's goal function, because it makes it worth our while to work hard on this project and increase our chances of landing the next project. Oh, and that solves Chambers' problem—because it won't cost any money."

"What, grades like those we get in high school?"

Danielle and I sit in silence for a moment. "Not exactly," I finally say, "our grade needs to reflect each company's contribution to the project's goal function. Since the two most damaging aspects to projects are usually changes and delays, I think the grade should be awarded on the basis of preventing such changes and delays."

"Hold on, you'll still give Danielle work regardless, right?" Ashley challenges us. "I mean, she is your sister."

"I give her work because she's an excellent designer, Ashley. Regardless of the fact we grew up together."

"And say she wasn't so great," she goes on, "would you give up helping your sister for a designer who might do a slightly better job?"

"Are you doubting my integrity, Ashley?"

"Of course not, Dad. I just think that just like teachers have favorite students who always get a slightly better grade, so will the grades you give be influenced by other considerations. Like if the designer just so happens to be your sister, for example."

"The kid's right," Danielle says what I myself am thinking. "I think your challenge will be to find objective criteria, which could quantify the performance of everyone working on the project. Something that will disregard any personal relationships, or even intrigues, and express only contribution to the goal function."

"That's obvious. If such a grade would be based on personal affinities or disdain, it wouldn't be worth the paper it's written on."

"But Dad, you yourself have told me a thousand times—there's no such thing as objectivity. Everyone sees things differently. You can't detach emotions completely."

"I'm afraid it's even worse than that," Danielle adds. "If some designer or contractor should feel that they're losing projects because they received a bad grade in bad faith, they would immediately run to court and get an injunction against your grading system. That would kill the system before it even begins."

I don't have anything to say in reply to that argument.

"Listen, it's not a perfect plan, but if we succeed in establishing objective criteria to measure the contribution of contractors, designers, and project managers to the goal function, then we would have a tool that would tie the project's goal function to the goal functions of those who plan and execute the project. The less subjective these criteria are, the more effective they will be."

"Maybe you need to find some sort of algorithm to award the grades, without any human intervention. That would resolve the risk of getting sued for being biased," Ashley proposes.

"That sounds like enough for one conversation," Danielle concludes. "You need to find a way to define these criteria. I think you have a lot to do."

I agree with her.

When Ashley gets up to serve a lone customer his cup of coffee, I look at Danielle.

"You know," I say, "the year before Dad died, during one of the nights I spent sitting by his bedside at the hospital, he told me he used to treat you like a little girl until one day when you explained something to him that he thought he would never understand. He never told me what that something was, but he said that since that day, your relationship was transformed forever. I think that's how I feel about Ashley now. I don't think I can see her as just a little girl anymore, after this conversation."

"I remember that conversation," she replies, "I remember exactly what that something was, and I totally understand what you're saying."

On the way to parking lot, I still run the last thing Ashley said through my head, almost without thinking. *An algorithm to award the grades, without any human intervention.*

# 29. RESOLVING A FAMILY PRISONER'S DILEMMA

For three full days, I embodied the cliché of a brokenhearted teenager. I couldn't bring myself to do anything but mope around on the couch, staring at my phone. Things between me and Sally were so sensitive, that I wasn't sure whether I did or did not want to see a text message from her pop up on my screen. We both felt we were teetering on the edge of a precipice.

I gave the boys my credit card and told them to order in whatever they wanted to have for dinner. After some strong words from Ashley, they even gathered up the mess they left behind and restored a semblance of order to the house. I still came into work, and despite some of the employees noticing dark rings under my eyes, no one said a word.

Sally and I did not pose an ultimatum to each other, but the toxic dynamic of our fight led us to entrench in our own positions. I could understand her desire to remain in the kingdom she built for herself, but I couldn't accept being the only one who had to make sacrifices—as if my and my children's desires and interests were negligible. Two forces were at play here—emotions and reason, and they both needed time.

Danielle once told me that when she works on a design and reaches a dead-end, a creative block in her case, she just drops the matter for a couple of hours, and the breakthrough usually comes by itself later. I went to sleep feeling that something like that had to happen, that it couldn't be that our love—yes, it's love, there's no arguing about that—would simply collapse at the face of its first major obstacle.

This morning, with Chambers, Greg, and Naomi at our weekly meeting, I got a notification on my phone that I had received a text message. Out of habit, I picked up the phone to see who the message was from; when I saw the name *Sally*, my heart skipped a beat. I quickly put down my phone, hoping no one noticed, and tried my best to settle back into the meeting. I have no idea what was said during those remaining twenty minutes, as I sat there in the meeting, blankly nodding along, my thoughts focused completely on the little cellular device in my pocket.

As soon as the meeting was over, I hurried to my office to check my phone and preparing myself for any scenario. Sally is certainly assertive enough to end things, and she knows very well how to express her thoughts. That's part of the reason why I fell in love with the woman. When I finally opened the message, I saw just two words: "Let's talk."

The ramshackle diner at the BP gas station has become a kind of an inside joke. We decided to meet on "neutral ground," and that place, situated conveniently halfway between our houses, fitted the bill. Besides, the food there is so bad, there's no way it will distract us from the important matters we have to discuss.

"Wait, wait, let's not get carried away," she stops me from kissing her when we meet, and somehow, I feel a deep truth beneath the amused tone. I don't know how many times she's been hurt by failed relationships, but it's clear I'm not the only one who was afraid to put his heart on the line.

We sit there for three hours. I have two cups of coffee and

a bottle of beer, Sally has three glasses of iced tea and an truly inedible salad, which remained there half-eaten on the table as a witness to our conversation, until the waitress finally put it out of its misery and threw it to where it belonged in the first place.

Had someone observed us from outside, they probably wouldn't be able to decipher whether we were negotiating a business deal or about to declare our love for each other. Sally is focused and decisive as she always is, but I know her well enough by now to notice the tiny twitches she gets in the corner of her left eye when she's nervous.

Even though we both know exactly what the other person thinks and feels, we don't spare the introductions. I tell her again the story of me and Karen's breakup and the process the kids underwent—this time without exaggerations—about the resultant changes in my life, and the endless joy I've felt since I've met her. I make it clear to her that I don't intend to lose her over a logistical matter, but I explain my children's needs and how relocating would be wrong for them. She, on her end, apologizes that her private fantasy about sharing her life with me led her to plan our dream house without asking me my opinion on the matter. She even manages to surprise me. "I want to tell you that I spoke with Bianca and Aaron before I came out here," she says and I tense up, "they both supported me, and Bianca even told me that out of all the people I've dated since the divorce, you're the only one she's genuinely liked."

I'm happy to hear that. We may be the ones in a relationship, but there are more than just the two of us to take into consideration.

This square can't be rounded—we have two homes, two families, five children, two exes, two new partners and their children, and every decision affects everyone. We agree that our goal is to live together from now and forever (yes, yes. I'm the first to say it, and Sally readily concurs.) We even agree that when we do live together, it will be good for the children, so we try to ask ourselves what everyone else who is involved in this story's goals are, and whether some of those goals could be sacrificed for the sake of our own. Finally, we conclude that, at this stage of our lives, uniting our houses into one household would require too great a sacrifice for one of the families, which would breed discontent and potentially lead to future arguments. We even agree on a timeframe. Six years. Until the last of the kids goes off to college.

"Maybe we should just move in here, in the middle," I suggest with a smile, but Sally doesn't laugh. "Maybe it's like Randy White's story," she says. "We already know where we want to go, but we have to take into consideration everyone else's goal functions, otherwise they would undermine our project."

After agreeing in principle, there's just the matter of logistics to settle. We play around with the days; Sally agrees to swap the mornings that she usually goes swimming, and even looks online to see whether there are any good Pilates places around my house.

In the end, we agree on what seems like the best compromise for now. We'll change the status of this relationship from *love affair* to *shared life*, but we'll each stay with our own kids in our own houses, and the other would come stay over. We agree upon fixed days for each family, for get-togethers and dinners with the kids, and even agree on a semi-annual vacation for all of us—two adults and five kids.

"So, what do you say?"

"I say, it's not what I dreamed of, but it seems like the best option we have for now," she smiles. "If I were managing a project, I'd probably describe this as the best arrangement to maximize our common goal function. In any case, you're not going to disappear on me anytime soon, right?"

"Me? Disappearing is your thing."

"Eric."

"Okay, okay. I'm not going to disappear on you."

"So, we have some time to see how this arrangement works for us, but I'm letting you know right now—I'm not going to spend the rest of my life waking up without you beside me."

"Can I get that in writing?"

"Of course, sir," she leans in and kisses me gently. Done deal.

We're now back at my place, in a completely different atmosphere. There she is, stepping out of the shower.

## 30. NO INFO, NO WIN

As soon as the meeting with Randy White at the DOT concluded, I picked up the phone and called Ethan to explain the situation. As I expected, he was very glad to hear about our mounting pressure. Every contractor knows that when there's pressure to make changes, the purse strings loosen.

"Start by doubling shifts and equipment, then drawing up a summary of the costs. I'll send you these instructions in writing in ten minutes, together with a guarantee the DOT will pay for all these expenses, along with an added twelve percent. Don't wait for any other confirmation. Just get every crew and piece of equipment you can get your hands on to the site as early as tomorrow morning—including from our other sites and from subcontractors."

As I spoke, I noticed I said *our sites*. I realized that I still identify with my previous job no less than I do my current one.

"Get Dr. Silver to the site today, and don't let him leave until he draws up a new plan that sees us wrapping up the project in five months' time." I added a small two-week buffer, hoping it would be enough.

"And make sure you have on-site everything you will possibly need to execute the plan."

"Aye, aye, sir," he answered jokingly, alluding to the reversal of roles between us. "Consider it done."

"Oh, and tell Randy White to include in the summary of costs any extra expenses to the subcontractors. I don't want anyone withholding their equipment because they're afraid they won't be paid for it."

All of that happened three days ago. Now, I'm on the site, sat in Ethan's Land Rover, with a strong feeling of déjà vu. We drive slowly along the road and look at the work taking place. The number of workers and heavy machinery is truly remarkable, and I ask myself—how did he pull this off in three days? I feel again what I've always felt about this man and his exceptional skills.

"Like the good ol' days, huh?" he says.

"Like the good ol' days," I reply.

We finish the tour and head back to the office. The detailed plan is hung up with three colorful pins on the conference room wall. Three sixty-by-forty-inch paper sheets, detailing all seven hundred and four activities remaining to be completed until the road is finished. Every activity is marked as a thick line, with thin lines connecting it to other activities which need to be finished before it can be started. Another set of lines connect it to other activities which can begin only when it is finished. Some of the activities are marked in red ink—those are activities on the critical chain, activities which, if they are delayed, would delay the project in its entirety.

Most people who encounter a schedule flowchart for the first time can't help but be impressed by its complexity. Usually, they assume that the person who drew up the schedule and updates it is a very smart individual who keeps a detailed picture of the project in his mind.

In contrast, people who work with schedule flowcharts on a regular basis tend to be much more skeptical. Ethan is among those skeptics.

"What do you want to do with these bedsheets?" he asks, pointing a dismissive finger toward the three hung sheets of paper.

"Actually, I just wanted to see that they exist," I answer. I walk up to the bottom left corner of the first sheet, which has its print date. It's the thirtieth of the previous month, some three weeks ago, before anyone knew there would be a new schedule and that the project's duration would be cut in half.

"You know me, I'm one of those who prefers bits over papers," I reply. "Do you have anything more up to date than this on your computer?"

"Even when we used to work together, computers and schedules were your thing, not mine," he answers, "but I asked Dr. Silver to come in. He'll probably have answers to your questions."

Five minutes later, Adam Silver walks into the room. He shakes my hand with a cordiality reserved only for individuals who can get him on the DOT consultants list.

"How are you, Mr. Price? I hear you're moving up in the world."

After thanking him politely, I ask to see his updated work schedule. He connects his laptop to the HDMI cable, and within a minute or two, we see the new schedule workflow on the 62" screen with 4K resolution hung on the opposite wall. "Should I walk you through the changes I made to the plan?" he asks.

"I don't have time for that," I tell him. "Let's just look at the key points. When's the finish date?"

He scrolls to the end, and points to the bottom

line—*Inauguration of the Road*. The date is five months minus four days from today. "Now show me your resource load chart."

He changes the screen, going over all the types of machinery and workers involved in the project. Excavators, compactors, shovels, trucks, graders, electricians, and so on. For each one of them, he presents the number of units needed per day versus the number existing in practice. There is not a single piece of equipment whose required amount exceeds the number we have on-site. Just like during the tour, I'm impressed again by Ethan's ability to get such a substantial amount of resources on-site in so little time.

"As you can see," Silver says, "there are quite a few days where the amount of equipment on the site far exceeds its requirement. This is a direct result of the dense scheduling. The logical dependencies between different activities don't allow us to keep a consistent workload for all the resources, and to ensure we finish on time, I had to schedule a large number to be on-site at the same time—but not all of them will always have work to do."

This was expected, of course. When I ask him to approximate what percent of the total equipment will stand idle at any given time, he answers that it's approximately thirty percent. I run the numbers through my head quickly and announce, "There are about fifty million dollars' worth of activities left. The resource component—the workers and equipment—amounts to about forty percent of that, meaning, about twenty million dollars, thirty percent of which is idle because they don't have work to do at any given moment. Thirty percent of twenty million dollars is six million dollars of real added expenses, which Randy White will be able to pump up to eight million dollars to be paid for by the DOT out of all of our tax-paying pockets. Not an insubstantial amount. But, on the other hand, that is significantly less than the cost of six months of a traffic jam at a rate of thirty-six million dollars a month.

"Say, Adam," I turn to him, "how do you make sure everyone knows what they have to do?"

"Actually, it's much simpler than any other project I've worked on so far," he answers. "Because you have so much resource surplus, crew managers come to me almost every day to ask where they can operate their crews. So, I'm on top of everything all the time."

"Mr. McKay," the site secretary walks into the conference room before Silver can finish his sentence, holding Ethan's phone which he left outside, as he always does, "there's a call for you. I told him you're in a meeting, but they say it's urgent."

Ethan is on the phone for two minutes, before saying, "I'll be there, goodbye," and hanging up.

With twenty years of reading Ethan's expressions under my belt, I immediately ask, "What happened?"

"They shut us down on the way to Brown Farm," he says.

Ronald Brown is a former Silicon Valley hi-tech entrepreneur who used the money he made after selling his company to buy an organic farm. Over time, he became an activist and a representative of all the independent farmers in the area against the large agricultural corporations and against globalization in general; he specializes in bringing together large crowds of farmers to demonstrate, stopping traffic by pouring milk on the road, and blocking entrances to super-markets that choose to sell corporate produce over locally sourced vegetables. A beat-up old dirt road leading to the farm was used almost exclusively by him and his family; the 612 cuts through this road, and the matter was sorted out only after the DOT guaranteed to build an alternative road by his approval before blocking the existing road. Yesterday, Ethan sent over an excavator, shovel, and six trucks which began work and blocked the old road. Needless to say, no one saw to the matter of the alternative road beforehand, which of course did very little to reinforce whatever little trust Mr. Brown has in the central government. Consequently, there are now two hundred men, women, and children from every farm in the region blocking the site, with others still arriving to join them. Ethan apologizes and rushes over to his car to try to talk his way out of this conundrum.

I stay behind with Dr. Adam Silver and try to work out how these events will affect his plan.

"Tell me, don't the road and the alternative road appear in your schedule?" I ask.

"Of course they do," he quickly defends his work, "here they are." He runs a quick search on the software, and the two activities pop up immediately. Opening the new road should have happened two weeks ago and closing the old road just slightly after. Neither one of them was on the crit-ical path. "That was Ethan's responsibility," he says, "but I guess he must've forgotten about it."

"How exactly was he supposed to remember it?" I find myself jumping to the defense of my former boss, "You know very well he doesn't read schedules, nor does he have any time for that with all his other responsibilities. Don't you have some system in place which directs every activity that needs to be done to the person responsible for executing it?"

"Not really," he says. "Like I told you before, heads of crews and project managers usually know more or less what they have to do, and they come to me only for updates."

I notice the slight difference between his current explanation and the more optimistic explanation I heard from him a couple of minutes ago, and I can't help but recall what Randy White explained to me in our first meeting. "Schedules are only good for claims. No one really uses them to execute the projects." I was mad at his cynicism then. Now, I start to fear that he wasn't being cynical at all. This is the most important project we've worked on for the past decade—if an activity was overlooked here because no one bothered to check their schedule, one can only imagine what goes on in other, less focused projects.

"We filed a request for information on this subject about a month ago," Kevin, the project manager, who just walked into the room to grab his phone that he forgot here before, jumps into the conversation. "We reminded the DOT that according to the project's specifications, we couldn't close one road before opening the other, but the alternate road is outside the range of our project and needs to be executed by a different contractor."

"And what answer did you get?" I ask him.

"I don't think anyone answered," he replies.

"Who was supposed to answer? Rodriguez?"

"Of course. He's the one who answers all of our requests for information."

A quick phone call later, I learn that Rodriguez forwarded the email and passed the question about the alternate road on to Ms. Marconi—the DOT's in-house contractor supervisor—the very day he received it.

Another phone call later, it turns out Ms. Marconi got back from her annual vacation only two weeks ago and has been so flooded with all the work that accumulated while she was away, that she hadn't found the time to answer the question.

I guess my anger is evident over the phone, since the call ends with Ms. Marconi saying in an unmistakable tone, "But Mr. Price, how in the world was I supposed to know that that stupid dirt road was more important than the seven hundred other emails I had waiting for me after two weeks off? How am I ever supposed to know what's more important than what, for that matter? I did the best I could. I solved the problems that were easier to solve first, and within a week I narrowed the opened emails list down from seven hundred to fifty. Then, I started working on the heavier cases in chronological order. I would have reached your dirt road within a day or two, even without your call."

Defeated and angry, I apologize for the tone of my voice and end our conversation. She really did upset me, but it wasn't her fault. She really didn't have any way of knowing what to prioritize.

I leave the site and head west. It's the longer route, but this way I can get a look at a stretch of road I didn't pass through when I came in a couple of hours earlier. I'm hungry and tired, so a full minute passes by before I notice I'm driving along a nearly abandoned road. The large number of heavy machinery I was so pleased to see this morning gave way to an empty expanse broken only by the sight of one lone excavator along a full mile-long stretch of unfinished road. I'm tired of this by now, but I can't help it; I call Adam Silver who is still in front of an open computer on-site and ask him if, according to his schedule, there shouldn't someone be working on sections 404 to 500 right now.

"Of course there is. The middle layer of asphalt crew should be there, two lighting crews, and four molding crews to prepare the castings for the drainage pipes," he answers.

"Well, they're not here," I tell him and hang up the phone.

A quick conversation with Kevin resolves the matter; thanks to the resource surplus, he was able to finish this whole section ahead of schedule.

"And who knows about this? Why didn't Adam direct the upper layer of asphalt and the landscaping crews over here?"

"I have no idea. We reported it in the work log, just like we do every day."

I swear this will be the last work call of the day. I have Adam on the line again, and I can hear by the tone of his voice that he's not very happy to hear from me again, either.

"According to the contract, we need to submit an updated schedule once a month. So, prior to making the monthly update, I go over the work logs and report the progress made based on what's written there," he explains.

"So, in other words, your schedule is synched, on average, to two weeks ago?" I repeat the obvious.

"Actually, more like three weeks," he answers, "because a couple of days go by from the time I pick up the work logs to the time I type them up and submit an updated schedule."

"Meaning that most of the time, if someone finishes their work ahead of schedule, the person who needs to follow him doesn't even know about it?"

"They usually do know about it because they meet at the site and talk to each other."

"If they know about it anyway then why do we even need your schedule updates?" I start to lose my patience.

"If you don't have an updated schedule, how can you file a claim against the owner for delays?"

## 31. REWIRING A MINDSET

I ask to schedule my meeting with Jill Sommers as early as possible. So when Dianna, Chambers' secretary, informs me that Jill will come in to see me at 7 a.m., two full hours before work at the DOT officially starts, I can have no complaints. I arrive at 7 a.m. sharp, only to see Jill already waiting for me in my office.

I tell her briefly about what I saw at the site yesterday, and finish with a request that the information systems department, which she heads, prioritize the 612 over any other project.

"Prioritize in what way?" she asks, as if she has no idea what I'm talking about.

"In every way. There isn't a single spare day on this project. We can't waste any time on mistakes. We can't have someone hold back their work simply because they don't know that the previous activity has been finalized. We can't have a request for information which is on the critical chain not attended to simply because no one knows it's on the critical chain, and we can't have someone working on non-critical activities when there are critical activities waiting, simply because he doesn't know which of his activities are critical. In short, we can't have lack of information causing delays to this project."

"But what does that have to do with us?" She isn't playing dumb. She genuinely doesn't understand.

"You're the information systems department. Provide the

information. If you don't have software that can do it automatically, then have two people do it manually. It's important enough, believe me. I'm sure you don't want to see three-hour traffic jams all across the country and demonstrations in front of the DOT offices, just because someone didn't know something that he could have known were he given the right tools."

"I don't think we can help," she says, "we don't have the tools for that. Even if I were to give you those two people, which of course I don't have, they couldn't help you, either."

The early morning hour and the coffee I've yet to drink make me less sharp than I'd like to be, and frankly, less friendly, as well. But Jill really is trying to help. She just doesn't know how to do so.

"You see," she goes on, "until our meeting with Randy White last week, we didn't even know there was such a thing as a project's goal function. And clearly, we didn't know that each of the other bodies employed on the project have goal functions of their own, that are so often in contrast with the project's goal function."

Well, I myself only discovered that recently.

"Even though many of our employees have read Goldratt's books, we assumed it was different in our field. We assumed that an accumulation of local improvements necessarily leads to global improvement, so we did everything we could to facilitate local improvements."

"What did that look like in practice?"

"We knew there are lots of types of information to be handled, but we thought that most of them are the project people's business, not ours. We thought that the DOT only cares about larger matters, like tracking the schedule and the budget. Therefore, we always let the project managers decide how to manage local information as they see fit."

"That's not necessarily a bad idea. That way, everyone works with the tools they know best," I say.

"Perhaps, but I guess the shortcomings overweigh the advantages. The result is that in every project, the contractor uses a local schedule software which we can't oversee. The person operating it is their own schedule expert, who just so happens to be their claims guy as well, and he is the only one who writes in it and reads from it. Usually, it ends up in claims worth millions of dollars. Against us, of course," she smiles bitterly.

"Schedules really are a problem," I say, "but what happens to all the other kinds of information?"

"The daily work reports are written by the contractor's site engineer in excel sheets which are then printed and signed by him and our inspector, so that all we are left with are paper logs. In terms of the availability of that information, we are basically no better off than we were in the old days when daily work reports were handwritten in three copies using carbon paper." I nod, and she continues.

"Contractors manage requests for information using one software, and requests for payments using another. They employ quality control companies to do quality control for them, each working with their own software, and work-meeting protocols are circulated in emails as PDF files. None of these programs are designed to communicate with one another, so, inevitably, they contain an infinite number of contradicting information."

"How do we get contradicting information?" I don't understand.

"When a contractor writes down what he's executed twice—once in the daily work report and once in the schedules—contradictions occur. When the project manager writes down problems that need to be addressed in the weekly meeting protocol, but the contractor writes down those same problems in the requests for information he submits, contradictions appear again. And there are loads of other examples."

"But why would any of them put down incorrect information?"

"I can only guess that when there are conflicts of interest among the writers, each one writes down whatever suits his agenda."

As a contractor, I of course know how things are run, but for some reason, I assumed that things are different for project owners. Now, it all sounds so low-tech—as if we were working with paper files and making calculations with an abacus. Suddenly, a new idea springs to my mind, and I immediately run it by Jill.

"Tell me, is it possibly you're exaggerating a bit? In the two months I've been here, I've read dozens of computerized reports, all of which were made using your information systems, which taken together contain a massive amount of information. I don't recall seeing even one piece of contradicting information. Maybe the problem isn't that serious, then?"

From the way she looks at me, I understand that I don't know what I'm talking about. "None of the reports you've read stem from raw data," she says. "Since the information isn't linked, and since the administrative reports require clear and coherent information without contradictions, we've given up on using raw data. Our entire information system is based on reports composed by project managers. We've created a special page listing all the details we care about, and once a month, each of them is required to report to our system about the different projects they manage."

"And what's the problem with that? Data is data. Why should we care who types it in?" I struggle to understand her point.

"There are several problems. The first problem is that project managers report only once a month, so our information isn't up to date. The second problem is that when they report a month back, they often don't remember exactly what happened, so the information is inaccurate. The third problem is that when we're talking about events that reflect they have done a poor job, they have an incentive to embellish the facts to make themselves look better, meaning the information itself is often distorted. Taken all together, there isn't any information in our information system that aids decision-making. What we have is information that explains decisions that were made beforehand. These decisions were based on the day-to-day data of the project itself. Data that doesn't even exist in our information system."

"And you mean to tell me that there isn't even one computer whiz in the entire DOT who could find a more elegant solution? Something to link all that data together?" I persist.

"Last year, some of the contractors started using a new software that united the daily work reports, the requests for information, and the requests for payments. But it made very little difference, because they continued to act as three different disconnected modules in that one software."

"And what does all that mean in practice?"

"It means that even in a case like the 612, where everyone wants to go the extra mile because they know we're willing to pay them a ton of money to expedite their work, they don't know how to do it. They can't tell what's urgent from what's not, or what's important from what's trivial. A subcontractor who does the work in practice doesn't even know which of his activities are on the critical path. The designer who needs to come up with solutions for problems doesn't know if a problem is urgent, or if he can take his time with it. The contractor's engineer reports his activities daily in his daily work report, but the schedule is only updated once a month, so most of the time the work plan is completely out of sync with reality…"

"Wow," I jump in as she pauses to inhale. "What you're saying is that a large part of what we call project management is in fact just manufacturing worthless documents and reports?"

"I would even say that that's being overly optimistic. I think they have plenty of worth—but almost exclusively for contractors when they prepare claims against us. Out of curiosity, after our last conversation with Mr. White, I inquired to see how much improvement we've made in keeping our schedules over the past fifteen years. What I found out is that the length of our delays has pretty much doubled over this period, and that the amount of changes increased by a similar scale. In every single parameter I checked, not only have we not improved—we have deteriorated. At first, I thought that couldn't possibly be correct, but then I read the McKinsey report, the one Randy White showed us in our last meeting. It turns out that it's the same situation across the entire field—in every county, in every continent."

"Did you report this to anyone? Or did you just find all of this out this week?"

"I've suspected parts of it for a long time now, and even brought it up with Naomi Griffin from legal, who tried to help. To stop the torrent of claims against us, she added a clause to the contract, stipulating, that aside from updating dates of execution, the contractor won't be allowed to make any change to the schedule without receiving our consent first. The result was that within two months, schedules no longer reflected reality."

"That's exactly what Randy White explained to me not long ago," I say.

Jill nods along. "You probably won't be surprised to hear that as a result of that clause, we started getting claims filed against us by contractors complaining that we prevented them from making necessary changes to schedules and thus hindered their ability to do their job." It looks like she came prepared for this meeting. Furthermore, it looks like she's been waiting a long time for someone to dig into the matter and shake up the current state of affairs. "You see, without a goal function, our orientation simply can't be right. And if we define the increase of the project's value as our goal, then we inevitably have to start from the ground up and rebuild our entire information systems to support that goal. To increase the project's value, we have to be able to provide credible, easily accessible, and non-contradictory information. That means no software can work in isolation from other software that influence the goal function. The daily work report should update the schedule. Requests for information should help manage their inherent risks, decisions in protocols cannot be conducted in disconnect with the correspondences based on which they were made, and document and plan management cannot be modules isolated from the rest.

"Oh, and I forgot the most important thing," I had tried to squeeze a word in, but she's not done. "The main challenge is that it has to be one system that everyone uses exclusively. The contractors, us, the designers, project managers… Everyone."

Even without being an information systems guy, I understand that she means a system to encompass practically every aspect of every project.

"One Ring to rule them all…" I quietly quote *The Lord of the Rings*.

She looks at me in surprise. "…*One Ring to find them, One Ring to bring them all and in the darkness bind them…*" she completes the quote with a little smile.

I didn't a say a word throughout her long monologue, but I understood what she said. Just to be certain, I ask, "How long would it take you to develop such a system?"

"In theory, something like three or four years." I see in her eyes that she's aware that, for all intents and purposes, she might as well have said a hundred years. But she then adds, "In practice, though, maybe never. It requires a complete rewiring of our mindset. We would have to make so many radical changes to our worldview and how we go about our work today, that I'm not sure we would even know how to do it at all."

I've stopped counting the amount of times this project has led me to a dead-end. What's one more...

But then she says, "There's an Israeli startup that has apparently developed something like that. They're the ones who came up with the idea of a project's goal function that we heard from Randy. I found them on Google after our meeting with him. Their idea combines Goldratt's theory of constraints with Nash's game theory. As far as I understand from their website, they claim that a project's goal function is more than just the only way to maximize its value—according to them, reorienting every participant's goal function to align with the project's goal function is the only theoretical solution to the problem of inherent conflicts of interest among its participants. Here, check them out if you're interested."

She ends the conversation by handing me a sheet of A4 paper with a web address written on its letterhead:

**www.actechway.com**

## 32. FIXING THE CONTRACTS

I set up a one-on-one meeting with Naomi Griffin, but at the last minute, I decide to invite Raji Umair to join us. Naomi's room is the best corner office on the third floor, the only one with an expansive view, and the only one as big as Chambers' office. In fact, it is located directly one floor below it. When we get there, I see she's not alone in the room, Katelyn Carner, Naomi's deputy in the legal department, sits on a chair next to her, at the low round conference table. The low table—meaning she's prepared to have a genuine conversation, rather than simply blow us off in a couple of minutes.

"I see you didn't come alone, either," she says when we walk in. "Good. I asked Katelyn to join me, as well. I think the subject you'd like to talk about warrants another opinion, and Katelyn's opinion often differs from mine."

After Naomi's secretary takes our order of hot beverages, I open the meeting. I explain that in continuation of our meetings with Randy White, I'd been trying to map the conflicts of interest that prevent us from maximizing the value of our projects. I briefly relay the content of the designers meeting at the site of the 612—which seems like ages ago, now—and how the only thing every one of them worried about was covering their own hides. I also tell them about my meeting with Nick Waters, the wall contractor, who explained to me about the conflicts of interest between the general contractor and subcontractors, and why subcontractors disregard the general contractor's schedule. I tell of my meeting with Jill

Sommers, who explained to me that even our information is tainted by conflicts of interest, and that subsequently, even when we understand what we want, and define our goal function clearly, we can't actively pursue it because we don't manage the information necessary to do so. Finally, I even tell the story of Ashley and Jayden's prisoner's dilemma, and how Ashley managed to resolve it. I conclude by saying that I'm here to talk about the manager's dilemma.

"You see, the prisoner's dilemma stems from the fact that the prisoner is required to operate within a framework of rules which doesn't allow him to make the decision which benefits him. In contrast, the manager's dilemma is all about how to define good rules, rules that will allow participants to benefit when they make decisions in the best interest of the project itself. In an organization like ours, the place where most formal rules are established—the rules according to which participants calculate their steps—is your department. When you draw up a contract, it affects everyone's conduct, therefore—"

"Excuse me for barging in," Naomi, who has kept quite so far, says, "but with all due respect to us, I think you're overestimating us a bit. The DOT's rules are dictated by the state government, and even Capitol Hill, who define our role and authority through legislation. Other rules are dictated by the manager, who instructs us on our priorities and conduct. Even more rules are determined by the information systems department; it may not perceive its conduct as rule-making, but, in practice, once the information systems department can't provide certain information—as in the case you just described—it dictates de facto rules of conduct based on the absence of that information. And this is before we take into consideration project managers who establish their own rules of conduct in every project, or other infrastructure companies, local authorities, environmentalists, and everyone else—each with his own set of rules that they impose on us."

"You're absolutely right, of course," I say, "every one of the bodies you mentioned does indeed do everything you just described. But still, at the end of the day—if you exclude external parties we have no control over—the rest of the participants conduct themselves according to the contracts you draw up. I guess that's obvious in regard to the contractors, designers, and project managers we have contracts with, but it's a similar situation even with our in-house project managers and the information systems. Ultimately, everyone is conducting themselves in accordance with the contract which they are trying to execute. Subsequently, the rules of the game are drafted in your department."

Naomi and Katelyn stare at me without saying anything in response. Eventually, it's Naomi who breaks the silence, "Let's say, for argument's sake, that you're not completely wrong. Which rules that come from us would you like to talk about? We've already amended the matter of the rule of tendering, as we discussed with Mr. White. Is there anything else?"

"Naomi, I'm not here looking for a fight. I'm not looking to scapegoat you for the delays on the 612, or any other project, for that matter. I'm here to try to work out together with you how we establish our rules. How we run our contracts."

"Look, broadly speaking, it's simpler than you probably

imagine," Katelyn explains. "We use four templates for standard contracts. Each contract is amended with a couple of pages written by the project manager which define the special conditions of the particular project, conditions which are not covered in the template. And that's about it. We attach the drawings and the specifications drawn up by the designer, all the standard appendixes, and put it out for tender. I assume that if you look into it, you'll find that at least ninety percent of the total time needed to prepare tender documents take place in other departments. Our part is relatively technical and swift."

"And who draws up our standard contracts?" I ask.

"That's pretty standard, as well. Once every couple of years we look over the existing contracts, make a summary of all the claims we've lost over those years, and try to ascertain if there are any holes in those contracts which caused us to lose those claims. If we find any, we do our best to plug them."

"And this all takes place in your department alone?"

"Of course not. Unlike the impression you might have of us, we're team players. Drafts of our contracts are forwarded to be looked over and approved by all the relevant departments, which is practically every department in the DOT. Usually, we conduct several meetings to go over every department's comments, and we just draft the final result in legal terms."

That sounds okay, but then Raji intervenes and asks, "If you had to take the goal function into consideration as well, and the orientation toward maximizing the project's value, would you do anything differently?"

"I don't think so," Katelyn answers, "I can't see how what

we're doing now is not oriented toward maximizing the project's value. When someone files a claim against the DOT, we protect our legal position in court. In most cases, we're successful. Contractors have a success rate of barely twenty percent, so we win about eighty percent. That saves the DOT something like half a billion dollars of taxpayers' money per year. I don't think you could maximize the goal function much more than that."

She's probably right, but it feels like we're asking the wrong question.

"So, basically, every department passes on their requirements and specifications, and you just package it?"

"Exactly. They define the demands, and we package it."

"I would call that establishing a set of rules which help the local maximization for every department, but completely overlooks the needs of the organization as a whole—its goal function."

"How so?"

"Because the insurance department cares about the insurance requirements, the warranties department cares about the warranties, the operations department cares about lowering its own people's workload during construction—but who cares for the project itself? Who cares for maximizing the project's value?" I ask.

After a silence long enough for two sips of coffee, Katelyn takes up the gauntlet. "You know what, when you put it like that, maybe you're right, maybe no one cares for maximizing the project's value. It could be that the process we've been using to manage our contracts has been suboptimal. The thing is, I can't think what we could have done differently with the contract itself, and what's wrong with the current contract."

"You know, this reminds me of my first conversation with Naomi, on the day I started working at the DOT. How did she put it? Something like, *to avoid being deemed by court as the liable party, I draft contracts with the purpose of passing every possible problem that might arise on to the other party, and, if possible, to more than one party*. I still think now as I did back then, that even if that's good for winning a claim in court, it can't be good for managing a project."

"Why?" Naomi sharply interjects. "It's true. Many contracts today are drawn up intentionally vague in order to protect the owner and pass the legal liability onto someone else. It is drafted that way to help deal with the legal contentions we know for a fact are coming. Where is the problem in that?"

"I am extremely doubtful that passing on legal liability does in fact help with legal contentions, but you're the experts on that. However, the damage that does to the project's execution is quite clear and evident. Focusing on legal procedures rather than on management procedures has turned the schedule and daily work report from project management tools to contractor claim management tools. Thinking about potential court sessions has turned the site-meetings protocol from a tool to help share and manage responsibility into a tool to help ditch contractual obligations. And most importantly, focusing our efforts on preventing contractor claims made us substitute on-site solving of engineering problems with off-site legal so-called risk management. Instead of dealing with questions of what and when to execute, which can be resolved on the spot, we find ourselves dealing with what we should or should not say in order to strengthen our legal position."

"So what? What's the actual damage caused by that?"

"What do you mean?" I start to lose my patience. "That means that we effectively give up on real-time decision-making, decisions that improve the execution of the project, and subsequently *maximize its value*. We substitute them for retroactive decisions regarding questions such as how much is to be paid to whom, as a result of *not maximizing* the project's value. When we close the stable door, long after the horses have bolted, all that's left is to work out the price of the missing horses—that's where your legal skills come into play."

"That's quite a speech you gave there," Katelyn says. I think that despite her sarcasm, I've genuinely got her attention now. "I think you're wrong there. A substantial part of the fruits of our labor is the deterring effect it has on future claims. If it weren't known to everybody that we win eighty percent of our cases, we'd have to contend with three times as many cases, and over much larger sums. You have to understand—these are public funds. Money without a mother and father to protect it. The only ones who can guard it are us, the legal department."

"The bottom line is that I don't think there's any substitute for the work we do," Naomi adds. "I concede, though, that there are things we don't do at the moment that perhaps we should start doing. If you could focus on these, we might be able to find some common ground."

I get the hint and stop treading on her toes. "What Randy said was that we need to draft the contracts in a manner that helps maximize the project's value. In order for that to happen, we need to reward the project's participants for actions that increase its value. But at the moment, our contracts reward indecision over decision-making. Just like the example of the 612, where it was within every participant's ability to resolve the problem, but no one wanted to take up the gauntlet because it was not beneficial to their interests. The reason for that is the contracts we drew up, intended to shield ourselves from claims rather than promote an effective execution. That's what we need to change."

"Eric, you're talking in slogans. Change to what? What do we need to erase and what do we need to add to our contracts to improve them?"

Raji has been quiet for most of the meeting. Whether that's because he is a bit out of his depth in the room or simply because he's had nothing to say so far, his presence is hardly felt. Luckily for me, he now opens his mouth and starts talking, "I think Randy's said it already. We need to start by making it so that the contractor who wins the tender will be the one who offers the best combination of price, duration, and previous performance grade."

"Why previous performance grade?" Katelyn asks.

"The price and duration will define the cost and time he requires to execute the project, and previous performance grade will assess his chances of coming through on his guarantees. In such a case, the winner will be the contractor most likely to maximize the project's value."

"Impossible," Katelyn answers bluntly. "The whole idea of the law of tendering is to afford different contestants an equal opportunity to win project. Now you want to give some contestants a better chance to win than others. We're going to be buried under a mountain of claims if we do that."

"That's actually incorrect," Naomi suddenly interjects. "What you just described is not the core idea of the law of tendering, but only our erroneous interpretation of that idea. The true objective of the law is to obtain maximum value for the public, with the underlying assumption being that through a tender which gives every participant an equal opportunity, you can get maximal value for the public. As we know, that assumption is false, and its use places the contestants in a prisoner's dilemma, prompting them to act against the project rather than in its favor. The solution to these prisoner's dilemmas is to turn them into iterated prisoner's dilemmas. If every contestant knows that their chances of winning the next tender depends on the quality of service they've provided on previous tenders they've won, then high-quality service will extend from being our interest alone to being their interest, as well. The problem is not in the law of tendering itself. It's in the fact that we've chosen to interpret it without understanding the ramifications of the prisoner's dilemma, and without understanding that they can be resolved by turning tenders into iterated prisoner's dilemmas. No judge would overrule our tender if we can explain why the manner in which we conducted it is in the best interest of the public."

"Wow," Katelyn says. "I hope you're right. Otherwise, the two of us are going to be spending the rest of our time from now until retirement in court."

At that moment, I realize that Naomi and Katelyn are on board, and that we're all pushing in the same direction. If we manage to truly be on the same page and work together, the sky's the limit. I take advantage of the opportunity and add some engineering matters to our discussion.

"Plus, we need to stipulate that the contractor present a schedule, including a buffer the length of one-third of the project's total length. Then, for each month of the buffer he doesn't use, we divide one percent of the project's value between him, the designers, and the project manager. That way, he's incentivized to finish as fast as he possibly can."

"But if the added value to the project is one percent per month and we give away that sum, how is that worth our while?"

"Because the project's value is about double for us than it is for him, since it includes the cost of planning, managing, expropriation of land, and clearing existing infrastructures. So, when we pay the entire crew one percent of the contractor's project value, we still keep half of the profit."

"And how do we determine his performance?" Katelyn asks. I see that she is taking notes, with the full intention of incorporating our conclusions into the contract.

"His performance evaluation should be comprised of his adherence to schedules in past projects and the number of insubstantial claims he has filed against us," I reply.

"And do we already know how to determine this grade?"

"Actually, no, we don't. But I have a conversation scheduled for tonight with an Israeli company that has developed a cloud-based platform for project management. It claims that it has an algorithm that can do it based on work logs and project schedules stored on their cloud."

"Grading performance using an algorithm?" Katelyn asks. "If this is true, it's a major breakthrough. That would mean no one could dispute the grade's objectivity."

"Is that it?" Naomi asks. "Is there anything else?"

"Of course there is. The next thing is to align the designers' and project managers' contracts to our goal function. In reality, the contractor's buffer could be eaten up by events and circumstances beyond his control. If the designers don't provide answers to his questions on time, that could delay the entire project at the expense of his bonus. In order for that not to happen, we need to align the designers' goal function to our own. We need to pay them conditional bonuses which will decrease for each day of delay they cause on the project's critical chain."

"But do we know how to count those days and ascertain who's responsible at any given point? I mean, we have whole court hearings dedicated to solving these questions exactly."

"You're right. In this case too, according to their site, the Israelis know how to pin down the answer with precision, right down to the hour. I'll look into it, of course."

"And is that the only change that needs to be done to the design contracts?"

"No. We want to include one more thing in their performance grade, the extent of inaccuracies to their designs. The reason for that is that the less accurate the designs are, then more changes they require along the way. And the more changes we need to make, the likelier it becomes that we face delays and fail to finish the project on time."

"And how do you define design inaccuracies? That sounds like something that would be very difficult to quantify."

"At the risk of repeating myself," I say, "the Israelis say they have a simple way to do it…"

## 33. THE ISRAELIS

I have to wait until the end of the workday because of the time difference, and then two additional hours until their marketing director is available. At least that means I'm being taken seriously, meeting their marketing director and not a mere sales representative. I guess they can see that an annual budget of two billion dollars is not something to be taken lightly.

When the Skype connection finally stabilizes, I see that there are two people on the other side of the line. The marketing director and the sales director. After exchanging mandatory pleasantries, we introduce ourselves. Their accent is tolerable; not bad, even. But their names are foreign to me, and I can't memorize them. I privately name the left guy *sales executive* and the right guy *marketing executive.* Pretty soon though, I forget about their titles and just stick with *left guy* and *right guy.*

I tell them about the 612 without naming the project and explain the importance of finishing the project before the closing of the alternative road. I tell them about the problems and inefficiencies I saw in the field as a result of our faulty information system.

"How much time do you have left?" the left guy asks.

"A little under five months," I reply.

"And how important is it that you finish on time?"

"Very important."

"I mean, how much money would it cost you if you don't

finish on time?"

They cut straight to the chase. I ponder the matter for a moment, but then decide that I've got nothing to lose. "More than a million dollars a day," I say.

"Are you willing to make an effort to prevent those losses?"

"We'd do just about anything."

"Challenging," the right guy says.

"But possible," the left guy adds.

"Could you be more specific?" I ask.

"Sure," the right guy starts. "As you probably already know, all existing project management systems were designed for one interested party only, the one who buys the software— be that a contractor, a project manager, or a designer. As a result, they are designed to protect the interests of that interested party, alone. Our ecosystem is the first that is designed to protect the interests of *all parties involved* in the project. To do so, it is necessary that all the project's data will be managed in one shared work environment, updated and managed by all of the project's participants, the owner, the project manager, the designers, the general contractor, and even the subcontractors and other bodies with a vested interest in the project."

"Additionally," the left guy adds, "all the data managed in our system are linked so that a change in one piece of data automatically affects the other. For example, when you put down what you did in the daily work report, the schedule is updated automatically. That means that the schedule is updated daily, rather than monthly, as is usually the case. The result is that our system knows where everybody should be and what everybody needs to be doing at all times; on the basis of that information, the system sends reminders and notifications to everybody regarding the assignments and activities they need to do to benefit the project."

"Not only that," the right guy picks up again, "since our entire ecosystem was built around the idea of goal functions, our system knows how to manage notifications for each participant by order of urgency. It can tell between minor problems and major problems, and between urgent matters and matters that can wait."

"So each participant sees in your system both the project's goal function and his own?" I ask.

"No. They see what they need to do in order to maximize the project's goal function, and they can see immediately what's in it for them."

"Based on comparisons between what every participant is supposed to do and what they do in practice," the left guy jumps back in, "our system knows who contributes more to the project and who contributes less, and creates a grade evaluating the performance of each participant based on that information. When you use this grade as the basis for deciding which participants you will work with on future projects, or to whom to distribute bonuses on a current project, getting as high a grade as possible becomes everyone's top priority, thereby aligning the best interest of the project with the best interest of all parties involved in its execution."

This reminds me of Ashley's idea for the solution of the prisoner's dilemma. To be certain that I understand correctly, I ask, "Do you use game theory?"

"Of course," he answers. "Contracts, by their very nature, put all the participants in a prisoner's dilemma. It's often more advantageous for the participants to act in their own self-interest rather than the project's interest. The solution is to use the iterated prisoner's dilemma, adding into the participants' considerations the potential gains from future projects they stand to make if they support the current project's objectives."

"Not only that," the right guy says, "to prevent the motivation to cheat, the transparency in our system is nearly absolute. That means that when someone doesn't do their work on time—everyone immediately knows about it. For example, if a subcontractor who is supposed to work on an activity on the critical path doesn't start work on time, that very same day a notification is sent to him, to the general contractor, and to the project manager. Since no one likes to be the one who screwed up, everyone tries harder."

"But transparency isn't always an advantage," I try to pose a challenge. "My lawyers would be horrified by the very idea of full transparency. They would tell me that in order to retain the upper hand in the claims they manage for me, they don't want the contractor to have access to any information that is not essential for him to execute the project."

"Your lawyers are, of course, correct. The point is, though, that their answer is based on a local goal function. Your organization's goal is to build roads; your lawyers' goal is to win court cases. They want to be able to brag to their colleagues about all the cases they've won and how they've managed to protect you from contractor claims. That might be good for them, but it's not good for the project. What is good for the project is to avoid reaching court in the first place, and that can only be obtained through transparency. Your organization's goal function is the internal rate of return of the roads you pave; to increase the return, you need to build roads efficiently, and for that you need good decision-making. The faster decisions are made and the more solid the informational foundation they stand on are, the better they are. Credible, transparent, and easily accessible information is the key to making swift and accurate decisions. Indecision and creating legal expenses, for both you and your contractor, will only serve to diminish the value of your goal function. That's why you want to avoid them."

"So, what you're saying is that I should get rid of all my lawyers?" I say with a sarcastic smile.

"Of course not. They're the ones who will draft your new contracts for you. Contracts that will allow you to pay the contractor and the designers and the project managers on the basis of their contribution to the project's goal function. They're also the ones who will help you manage the processes of amending existing contracts during projects, without having to go to court."

I've sat with a sales person or two over the course of my life, so I know that in order to understand what it really is that they're selling you, you have to ask tough questions, the kind that reach a level of detail that sales people are not prepared for in advance. So I try a new direction. "The whole construction world today is going in the direction of BIM[3]

---

3    Building Information Modeling – A method of three-dimensional design that greatly increases the quality of design.

and Lean[4] systems," I say, "and your system completely ignores them. Does that mean that whoever buys your product today would have to shelve your system within a couple of years, because it will be out of step with the systems of the future?"

By the smile on their faces, I see that rather than probe at their soft spot, I've laid the ball up to them for a slam dunk.

"Lean *is* us," the left guy says.

"And we are the future of BIM," the right guy neatly concludes.

"You see, BIM systems provide excellent solutions for co-operation among designers. These are huge systems that do indeed allow for great improvement at the design level, but that's it. Only design. They're not meant to manage the operational stage, not to resolve the conflicts of interest between the project's different participants, and they're not meant to support the project's contractual conduct. In a deep sense—they are designed to greatly improve one aspect only, so the natural next step in their evolution would be to integrate into our system. That's the only way they can reach a full solution."

After a couple more attempts to find holes in their worldview, all of which are met with well thought-out and articulated answers, I ask what seems to me to be the million-dollar question, "How long would it take you to install this system for us?"

"We're a cloud-based ecosystem," the right guy says, "to

---

4    Lean Construction – A worldview aiming for efficient and waste prevention practices in the field of construction.

install, all we need is a list of the bodies and individuals involved in the project. That's it. We can do it in a day."

"But since we're talking about a project that's already ongoing," his colleague interjects, "we'd have to upload all the live data you have at the moment onto our ecosystem, schedule, requests for information, and open assignments. But if we forget about the rest—the documents and the designs—and if we all put in a great effort, we could do it in a couple of days."

"A couple of days?" Did I hear correctly?

"A couple of days," he says, and quickly qualifies his statement, "maybe a week."

"Are you sure? We can have the system up and running in a week? That sounds too good to be true." I feel like a drowning man who refuses to believe the lifeline he has just been thrown.

"Depends on your definition of *up and running*." It's the right guy, again. "The software will work in a week. But the software is only part of the system. To manage a project, you need to define its goal function and then align all the other participants' goal functions to it, so that it is advantageous for everyone to support the owner's goal. The software is only the first level, the one that facilitates the other two."

My feeling of confusion must be evident in my expression because the left guy quickly tries to help bring clarity to the matter.

"Your case is unusual, since the value of finishing on time is so high that the goal function can be simple, solely addressing time consideration and disregarding all other aspects. What's left is aligning everyone else's motivations to those of the project."

"Okay, so how do you usually go about doing that?" I ask, still unsure if I am excited or skeptical.

"Usually, we ask the client what he wants," he answers with a smile. "Most of our clients are companies like you, and the majority of them select the full solution. They use the mechanism embedded in our ecosystem to rank the performance of all the participants on their projects. They use the results of these ranks for two different purposes: the first, as a basis to distribute performance-based rewards, and the second, they use these ranks to prioritize bidders with higher rank in future tenders. There are several ways to do this, but the final result is that in order to secure for themselves a succession of projects in the future, all the participants work to the best of their abilities in the present."

"We also have a mechanism to rank everyone who works with us," I tell them, "for every project, we rank every participant based on ten different criteria which encompass their activities in the project. I'm afraid that despite the effort we invest in doing it, we have yet to find any meaningful way to apply the results of this grading mechanism. Our legal department claims that if we use it to choose between bidders on a tender, we open ourselves up to lawsuits for supposedly prioritizing our friends."

It looks like the left guy was just waiting for this question. "The biggest advantage of our mechanism is that the ranking is done objectively, almost entirely by a computer, with only negligible human intervention. Furthermore, we look at only one thing—the contribution of every participant to the goal function, making it clear to see why our ranking is relevant for selecting the participants of future projects. The result is that our rank is never questioned, and thus can be used without any problem."

"Why shouldn't we apply that solution to our project?" I ask, even though I think I know the answer.

"Because you're dealing with a project where all the relevant contracts have already been signed a long time ago," he gives the answer I assumed he would. "In order to change existing contracts, you'll need the legal department and the mutual consent of the other signatories of the contract, as well as their legal consultants. All that would take months, so that road is a dead end."

"What other options do I have?" I ask, not sure what answer I want to hear.

"I think that in your case, the best way to go about it is the classic way, allocate a couple of millions of dollars in bonuses paid to every participant who finishes his work on time. My estimate is that if you pay bonuses amounting to a quarter of the value of the work still remaining to be done, that should be enough to make it worth everyone's while to double their efforts. If you offer to pay bonuses, that would be a contract amendment no one would possibly refuse. Actually, in these cases, the best solution is usually to set a bonus for the project as a whole and let each participant know what percent of that bonus they stand to receive if the project concludes on time. Usually, that incentivizes all the participants to make sure their colleagues don't mess up and help each other wherever necessary in order to reach their shared objective of getting that bonus."

I remember the effort it took me to convince Naomi

Griffin to pay just three million dollars to expedite the project, so I quickly try to think what chance I have now in requesting three times that amount for the same purpose. "Is there a third way?" I ask.

They exchange glances, and finally the right guy says, "Actually, there is. In our experience, even customers who simply installed our system without using the ranking mechanism and without paying bonuses still achieved significant improvement in their results. It turns out that most people prefer working efficiently rather than inefficiently. So, when the system helps them know what they need to do and sends them reminders and notifications to help them do it, they tend to work better. Just having the transparency in place, which allows everyone to clearly differentiate between good work done punctually and poor work, makes them try harder. Furthermore, because everything is transparent and it's much harder to cheat, even those who may have tried to cheat without the system in place fall in line when they know the risk of getting caught is greater."

"So, what you're saying is that without amending contracts and without paying bonuses, in a week's time, I can have a system in place that will give most of what I wanted?" I try to find the catch.

"Yes," they exchange gazes. "That's what we're saying."

## 34. APPLYING THE SYSTEM

Once again, we're sat in Chambers' office, Chambers, Greg Nader, Naomi Griffin, and me.

"This is a follow-up meeting," he opens the conversation. "Over the past few weeks, we've had quite a few ideas tossed around regarding the task I assigned Eric when he first came into this office—to find a way to stop the flow of claims filed against us; to revert back from being lawyers to being efficient infrastructure builders. Eric, since each of us has only been exposed to part of the picture so far, why don't you tell us where things stand at the moment?"

I try to think where to start. I've had so many leads that led nowhere, it's hard for me to determine the correct chronology of events. I start by recalling, almost verbatim, my last phone call with Randy White. "Look," I say, "executing a road construction project, even the smallest one, requires the co-operation of a couple of dozen different parties: designers from about twenty different disciplines, a general contractor and subcontractors, a project manager, and several local authorities and public institutions. Each one of these parties has their own interests, which differ from those of the project itself…" I pause to let my introduction sink in.

"These conflicts of interest make it so that, all too often, a participant's rational course of action is in fact detrimental to the value of the project as a whole," I continue. "As a knock-on effect, the participants suffer from working in an environment that cannot pay high salaries, due to its low productivity. Despite the fact that the effect of these conflicts of interest are the most decisive factors in multiple-participant project management, project management theory doesn't even acknowledge them, let alone offer any kind of solution to the problem. What Randy White showed us was the missing link in project management theory—the problem of conflicts of interest, and their solution using the goal function. The conflicts of interest between the different participants in the project are a classic example of the prisoner's dilemma; to a great extent, each of these participants is a prisoner within a system where he alone cannot alter its rules."

"A prisoner within the system," Naomi repeats my words, "that sounds like the Matrix. Aren't you being a bit melodramatic?"

"Perhaps," I reply, "but the analogy to the prisoner's dilemma is the red pill which helps whoever takes it to understand how to escape the Matrix. The person who creates the prisoner's dilemma is the one who puts the two prisoners into a framework of rules he determines, according to which they make their decisions. In the prisoner's dilemma, the rules are such that when the prisoners act rationally; they achieve a worse outcome than they might have achieved under a different framework. Furthermore, the performance of the interrogator is bad as well, since he established a framework of rules in which both prisoners are likely to incriminate themselves, regardless of whether they are actually guilty or not. If he wants to know the truth—rather than simply get a conviction—he needs to change the framework of rules according to which the two prisoners make their decisions. In that sense, the prisoner's dilemma is a great analogy to the state of affairs at the DOT. You see, we're the ones who establish the rules according to which most participants in the project conduct themselves; therefore, we're the ones who can prevent the manifold prisoner's dilemmas we put our employees in.

"The rule-maker's dilemma is how to establish a framework in which the interests of his subordinates are aligned with his own." I look around the room to make sure I'm getting my point across. "The first thing the rule-maker has to do is define his goal function. This is the stage everyone tends to skip, out of a false assumption that the goals are so self-evident that there's no point wasting time defining them. As Randy White showed us, nothing could be farther from the truth. Even though so many of us deal in project management, none of us have ever tried to unify all our local goals into *one goal function*. As a result, our entire work doctrine is a patchwork of conflicting goals. Each one of these patches was created by people who, for all their talents and good intentions, strove to obtain a local goal that they perceived as important, without considering the needs of the system as a whole. Consequently, we drafted contracts that don't reward contribution to the project's value, we established schedules that make it impossible to conclude work on time, and paved roads according to principles belonging to the realm of legal argumentation. A clear definition of the goal function is the only thing that can remedy all these wrongs. The goal function is the key to everything we do from here on out.

"The goal function needs be written in big block letters and hung on every wall in the DOT, because it's intended not only for those who drafted it, but for all the people who need to put in work in order to maximize it. At any given moment, each can see his partial view of the picture, but in order for them to do their jobs in the best possible manner, they need to be able to answer the question: *is what I'm doing right now helping to maximize the goal function of the institution as a whole?* Like Randy White has shown us, our goal function needs to be the maximization of our projects' value, rather than simply keeping to their budget, quality, or schedule."

Chambers nods his head and mumbles, "Yes, yes, I remember that well. He dragged us all the way to the top of Everest to make that point."

"The next stage," I say after taking a small sip of my coffee, "is to provide each of the project's participants with clear instructions regarding what they need to do in order to maximize the value of the project. To do that, we need one single information system that manages all the data of the project. The system needs to be able to link the various data to each other, and be able to derive actionable insights from that data regarding what needs to be done, by whom, when, and at what cost. It needs to make the project's data transparent and easily accessible, and to notify the project's participants about which actions they need to take in order to maximize the project's value. It also needs to provide them with information about the scale of benefit or damage that will be done to the project if they do or do not finish their assignment on time. For example, it needs to alert a subcontractor that on Tuesday, he needs to start a certain activity which is on the project's critical path, and that if he doesn't start and finish the activity on time, he will cost the project thirty thousand dollars for each day's delay. In this manner, the subcontractor can compare between the cost of ordering a special piece of equipment or machinery necessary to complete the activity —say, at a cost of one thousand dollars—and the cost of thirty thousand dollars the project will incur if he doesn't do so..."

I take a short pause, and continue, "In such a system, all correspondence among participants will be managed in one place. All the data will be linked. The schedule will be linked to the work reports, and therefore always up to date. The system will send notifications to everyone regarding urgent activities they need to attend to, before neglecting them turns into a problem. That way, finally, we can have a schedule that is actually relevant to the work being done. On the other hand, in cases where necessary activities are not carried out properly, the system won't allow anyone to hide; the difference between doing your work and not doing it will become evident and transparent. All of these factors together will lead to a broad consensus about the facts, and significantly diminish a participant's ability to contest the validity of such facts. As a result, there will be less false claims, addressing the problem Chambers hired me to solve in the first place—"

Naomi Griffin barges into the conversation before I even pause to inhale.

"You're being overly optimistic. A real schedule and consensus over facts won't curtail contractors' motivation to file claims against us. That's how they make their living."

"I'm not being overly optimistic, but you are right that a real schedule and consensus over facts is not enough *in itself* to prevent false claims. For that, we need the performance evaluation grade. The system will take the data regarding the actions participants did or did not take and aggregate it into an objective grade for each participant based on their contribution to the project, or lack thereof. We'll use this ranking to distribute bonuses for good performance, and to select the participants with the highest grades for our future projects. I'll get to that in a minute."

"I can't wait..." Greg Nader mumbles. I see Chambers is nodding skeptically, as well.

"Even though the advantages of these changes are clear, they involve a substantial amount of difficulties. Designers, project managers, contractors, and managers of all rank within the organization could rise up and protest having their performance recorded and compared to that of others. Responsibility over actions, oversights, and failures will become much more evident, and the ability to dodge responsibility by pinning the blame on an external reason—like, *the electric company didn't relocate the pole on time*—will be significantly reduced. This will draw a clear line between individuals with the natural inclination to own up and shoulder responsibility for their actions, and individuals who make a habit of avoiding responsibility as much as they possibly can. Furthermore, this will turn indecision from acceptable practice to something that needs to be avoided; delays in decision-making in order to get a second or third opinion, or for the sake of conducting another discussion in a larger forum, will be viewed for what they actually are—delays that are detrimental to the value of the project."

"Come on. It's one thing to expect contractors and designers to conduct themselves with integrity because the system is transparent, but it's a different story altogether if you expect *us* to do so…" Naomi Griffin is half sarcastic and half serious. I take that as a sign of her appreciation of the scale of change I am proposing. The hard part still lies ahead.

"The next stage in the process," I say, "is the stage in which we change our contracts. This is relatively more difficult to do because it requires a complete rewiring of the mindset in all parts of our organization and even in external bodies we employ. Over the past few decades, the contracts governing the execution of projects have become increasingly complex, and so littered with legal jargon that they are impenetrable to anyone without legal training. As a result, a large part of the decisions that are taken in order to comply with the demands of the contract are based on legal counsel and opinion, which makes them appear to be indispensable. By their very nature, legal opinions take a long time to produce; the value of the project is seriously damaged by slow decision-making. Therefore, a more productive structure would be a structure in which the contracts are clear and simple enough to make obsolete the need for legal counsel and opinion in order to execute the contract."

Before Naomi has the opportunity to interject and explain to me why that's fundamentally impractical, Chambers intervenes and says, "That's not impossible. That's exactly how things were thirty years ago."

I'm on a roll now, and everyone in the room allows me to finish uninterrupted.

"While managing claims after events have already taken place, by its very nature is a zero-sum game, preventing such claims through legal means that necessitate decision-making in conditions of uncertainty is a completely different game. This *game* allows us to increase the pie, rather than simply deliberate how to divvy up the remaining slices after the project has already ended badly. These new legal capabilities, the ones we need to adopt, will allow engineers to maximize the value of the project in real-time, through swift decision-making under conditions of uncertainty."

Naomi waits for me to finish discussing the legal aspects and says, "I remind you that you still haven't demonstrated how you intend to decrease participants' motivation to file claims against us. Without that, we'll still spend all our time in court, and therefore continue drafting draconian contracts that will help us win, making all the changes you just discussed impractical."

That's encouraging. She's not against me, she's genuinely looking for a solution to change the motivation to file claims against us.

"Actually, that solution also stems from the prisoner's dilemma," I answer. "As you probably remember, the classic solution to the prisoner's dilemma is the use of the iterated prisoner's dilemma. When both prisoners know they will meet again in the same situation, they take into consideration not only their immediate gain, but future gains as well, so they opt not to incriminate each other. In our case, as well, most participants are recurring participants. If they'll know that their conduct on a particular project influences the prospects of winning future tenders, their motivation to file claims will decrease.

"For example, let's say that winning the tender will be based not only on who offers the maximal value for the project, but also the accumulation of his ranking on previous projects he's executed. Now, let's say that filing false claims is a criterion that lowers his ranking. In such a situation, before filing a claim against us, that contractor will ask himself, *is it really worth it?* Does filing a multi-million-dollar claim which might yield him a twenty percent settlement actually do him more harm than good by decreasing his chances of winning future tenders? I believe that in most cases, contractors would prefer to drop clauses intended solely to inflate the size of the claim and stick only to what they believe they truly deserve. In such a situation, we can drop the clauses that were only ever intended as a screen of legal vagueness to help us with these cases. The result will be a significant decrease in contractors' motivation to file inflated claims. I remind you—it's up to us to establish the rules, so it's within our ability to help those who work for us escape their prisoner's dilemma."

"You're not just talking about a different contract for the contractors," Naomi says. "You're talking about all other contracts with designers and project managers. That's no simple matter. You're asking to make a lot of changes at once. Do you have examples of such contracts?"

"No," I answer plainly, "but I don't think that's going to be a problem. The day I arrived, Mr. Chambers introduced me to the best legal consultant in the public service within a thousand-mile radius. She'll probably know how to draft them. Not only that, she will probably know how to construct our new rules of conduct for the duration of the project's execution and establish legal conduct on our part that will not require recourse to legal action on a day-to-day basis."

For a second, I think I've left her speechless. But twenty

years of legal battles must teach you how to regain your wits quickly. "Don't believe Chambers, he tends to exaggerate…" she says, and we all smile.

"That's it," I say, and turn to look Martin Chambers in the eye. "A final matter—or, rather a first matter—for all of this to happen, we need a leader. The kind of leader who dared believe that an engineer coming from the other side of the tracks could see things that can't be seen from this side, and who dared task him with an assignment that was way beyond his capabilities, but gave him the backing to pursue a solution. Now comes the hard part for you, as well. Now that we more or less know what the solution is, we need a leader to take the decision to implement it, with the full knowledge that about a million things are going to go wrong along the way. We've definitely overlooked some things here and there, and in the process of constructing our new rules, we are bound to come across them again, at which point we will have to take responsibility—say, *oops, we made a mistake*—and go back to the drawing board to correct it. It won't be pleasant, but it's necessary."

"Long story short," I conclude, "we need a leader who will take the task of implementing this massive organizational change on himself and assume responsibility for its results. A leader to say *this is the goal function*, and then say, *follow me!* Leaders like this are hard to come by. But the good news is that just one is enough, situated at the head of the pyramid, to influence and change everything below him."

"Alright, alright," he mumbles as he takes out a bottle of Scotch from his drawer and pours us all a round. "Stop kissing up."

## 35. FAMILY

"That was one of the weirdest weekends ever," Ben announces as we finish putting our luggage in the trunk and get in the car.

"Good weird or bad weird?" Ashley asks before I get the chance to ask myself. After thinking about it for a moment and exchanging a glance with his brother, he answers, "Good weird."

Honestly, that's not a bad way to describe what we've just experienced. Me and the kids, just us, a whole weekend at Sally's house. And while we're at her house, she and her kids are at our house.

It sounds like a lousy party game, but as soon as Bianca—her, of all people—suggested it, Sally and I jumped at the chance. Exchange weekend. "Make yourselves at home," a large card on the kitchen table read, beside a heap of snacks and soft drinks that Sally would otherwise never have brought into her house. I appreciated the gesture.

We spent the weekend exploring the area around Sally's house, picking herbs from the garden and even putting some of them in our morning omelets. It's been a long time since we had a chance to be together, just us, to fight and bicker, and to enjoy each other's company.

The agreement was that Sally and I won't talk to each other, won't call to ask where the television remote is or how to turn on the jacuzzi. Both of us had to feel at home, which meant acting completely natural. I bit my lip several times when Ben and Josh got into pillow fights, or when Ashley placed her dirty feet up on the couch—but a deal's a deal.

"I think it was really fun," Ashley says and smiles at me, "and I doubt this was our last weekend here. Right, Dad?"

Over the past year, I've gotten to know new sides of my daughter, her wisdom and maturity. I'm still excited, but no longer surprised by her words and actions.

"I agree," Josh announces, "it really was fun. Especially when we played football in her huge garden!"

I want to say that there are some things he should probably not mention in front of Sally, but I remind myself of our deal—*feel at home.*

"And besides," he adds, "I wouldn't mind coming back a few more times. I just hope they didn't mess up my room!"

"Mess up *your* room?!" Ashley cracks up, "You couldn't possibly make a bigger mess than it already is. Anything anyone would do in there would make it slightly tidier."

The kids, naturally, start bickering and teasing one another. I keep quiet as long as it's in good spirits. In the meantime, I turn the wheel to the right and turn toward the old gas station, kill the engine, and step out of the car. The kids have no idea what I'm up to.

"What now, Dad?" Ben says irritated.

"One last trip for the weekend, okay?"

The three of them are a bit grumpy, but they follow me along the path Sally showed me a couple of weeks ago. We enter the field and then the forest, and by the time we reach the clearing, everything is already set up: a large table, balloons, flowers, and food that covers nearly every inch of the checkered tablecloth. Sally, Bianca, and Aaron are already there, now walking toward us. Aaron goes over to the boys, Bianca and Ashley are already chatting, and Sally gives me a big kiss and a hug. "Well, how'd it go?" she asks, and I answer by simply smiling. "Us too," she says.

The boys pounce on the food. The girls join in and fill their plates, and only Sally and I are sitting to the side, contently watching the scene before us. I'm sure that she, just like me, is asking herself if one day, this group will feel like one big family.

"Isn't it amazing how many twists in the plot life throws at you?" she says and caresses my shoulder. "If you had told me a few months back, during our first meeting, that this is where we'll be in such a short time, I'd have called you crazy."

I reflect back on that meeting, on the big crisis I faced as manager of the 612 for Ethan, the high-voltage cable that was torn up and the urgent meeting with the designers; I recall Chambers' surprising offer, his frustration with increasing delays and mounting legal claims; my surprise meeting with Randy White and the series of lectures that followed, and our big breakthrough—and how throughout all that time, Sally and I grew closer and closer. It wasn't always smooth sailing, but now that these two ships have settled, they are sailing across calm and safe waters.

After everyone's done eating, Sally organizes the collection and separation of recycling goods, and I invite my kids to join me up the hill at whose base we are currently sitting. Huffing and puffing, we finally make it to the top, to find a lovely panoramic view of the area. It's getting darker, and the pesky sun is in our eyes, but between the brown-green fields before the horizon, we can clearly make out a bold black line.

"Is that your road, Dad?" Ben asks, and Sally and I smile at each other.

"Not mine, everybody's. But yes, that's the 612, thanks to which all of us will stop sitting in traffic one day, and also thanks to which we are all standing here together, now."

"When will it be ready?"

"If only you'd known how many people have asked me that question over the past year. I believe we'll be driving across it within two and a half months."

"Wow, I thought it would take longer," Josh jumps in, and reminds me of the day he tagged along with me to meet Ethan at the site.

"Many people did," I hug him, and look over at Sally. "I thought so too, myself. But I discovered that in order to reach better results, we need to rethink things we feel are obvious, and sometimes just dive into the deep end."

"Your father's a wise man," Sally turns to Ben and pulls me in tighter. Ashley and Bianca are already rolling their eyes, so we avoid a corny kissing scene. But as I hold Sally with my left hand, I reach into my pocket with my right hand, just to make sure. The ring is there.

## EPILOGUE

I established ACTech (Aligned Contracts Technologies) together with my partners a short while before embarking on writing this book. We established the company as a result of the insights presented throughout this book, in order to provide a new kind of solution to the world of large multi-participant project management, the kind I have been working on for the past thirty years. This chronological similarity naturally led to similarities between us and the different characters which appear in the book.

To a certain extent, we followed the paths of Martin Chambers and Eric Price, who sought to find a way to manage projects efficiently and without legal claims.

In a different way, we resembled Randy White, who discovered that each project decision can be made by following the answer to one simple question: what needs to be done in order to increase the project's value for its users?

On many occasions, we felt like Jill Sommers, who spent her entire career managing project data without knowing that the data is completely useless, since all decisions on the project are made without consulting it.

Quite often, we found ourselves in Naomi Griffin's shoes, the lawyer who drafts contracts designed to win cases in court, and for that very reason are wholly inadequate for managing the execution of projects, and do its value more harm than good.

Other times, we met and identified with the designers,

project managers, contractors, and subcontractors who found themselves repeatedly dealing with the question of whose benefit should they prioritize, the benefit of the project they were hired to execute, or their own.

But it seems that more than any character, we are those "Israelis" from Chapter 33, who explain what needs to be done so all of the project's participants can work in unison toward maximizing the project's goal function. Those who point to making the necessary link between increasing the project's value for its users and increasing its value for everyone who works to complete it; those who show how the conflicts of interest between the project and those who execute it can be resolved by switching from managing one-off prisoner's dilemmas to iterated prisoner's dilemmas.